W9-DEN-219

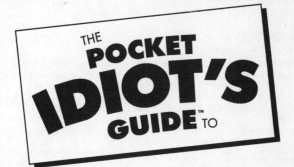
THE POCKET IDIOT'S GUIDE TO

Housetraining Your Dog

by Liz Palika

ALPHA

A member of Penguin Group (USA) Inc.

ALPHA BOOKS

Published by the Penguin Group

Penguin Group (USA) Inc., 375 Hudson Street, New York, New York 10014, USA

Penguin Group (Canada), 90 Eglinton Avenue East, Suite 700, Toronto, Ontario M4P 2Y3, Canada (a division of Pearson Penguin Canada Inc.)

Penguin Books Ltd., 80 Strand, London WC2R 0RL, England

Penguin Ireland, 25 St. Stephen's Green, Dublin 2, Ireland (a division of Penguin Books Ltd.)

Penguin Group (Australia), 250 Camberwell Road, Camberwell, Victoria 3124, Australia (a division of Pearson Australia Group Pty. Ltd.)

Penguin Books India Pvt. Ltd., 11 Community Centre, Panchsheel Park, New Delhi—110 017, India

Penguin Group (NZ), 67 Apollo Drive, Rosedale, North Shore, Auckland 1311, New Zealand (a division of Pearson New Zealand Ltd.)

Penguin Books (South Africa) (Pty.) Ltd., 24 Sturdee Avenue, Rosebank, Johannesburg 2196, South Africa

Penguin Books Ltd., Registered Offices: 80 Strand, London WC2R 0RL, England

Copyright © 2007 by Liz Palika

International Standard Book Number: 978-1-59257-684-5
Library of Congress Catalog Card Number: 2007928983

09 08 07   8 7 6 5 4 3 2 1

Interpretation of the printing code: The rightmost number of the first series of numbers is the year of the book's printing; the rightmost number of the second series of numbers is the number of the book's printing. For example, a printing code of 07-1 shows that the first printing occurred in 2007.

Printed in the United States of America

To Bashir, an awesome dog, my "heart dog" and the easiest dog I have ever housetrained!

Contents

Introduction

I have been teaching dog owners how to train (and live with) their dogs for more than 25 years. This is not just a profession for me; it's also a calling. My dogs are a part of who I am, a part of my family. When I can help people understand their dog better and teach their dog some manners, well, then that dog has a much better chance of living out his life with that family. Far too many dogs end up in shelters and rescues because they haven't been taught what are acceptable behaviors and what are not.

Problems with housetraining issues are not uncommon. Perhaps the new puppy doesn't understand what is being asked of her, or a newly adopted adult dog is lifting his leg on the dining room table leg. Or worse yet, a once-well-housetrained dog suddenly begins having accidents. Housetraining problems can drive a dog owner to distraction!

It doesn't help the dog owner when every dog trainer, and every dog training book, offers a different solution to the problem. If you listen to or read too many instructions, you and your dog both will be horribly confused. However, in this book I will create order from the chaos. I'll walk you through the process step by step and help you set your dog up to succeed. (My mantra: "Set your dog up to succeed!")

My dogs are therapy dogs and visit nursing homes and daycare centers. They must be well housetrained. In addition, my husband and I often travel with our dogs, staying in hotels and motels where accidents are unacceptable. My dogs were all house-trained using the same techniques I'm going to teach you. So continue reading!

Extra Help

Throughout the book there are three different types of sidebars. These offer tidbits of extra help to go along with the material in the text. Decoding them is easy.

All the Scoop

These boxes offer helpful hints about the housetraining process. You can find information about the time required to build a habit to the age a puppy can begin learning housetraining skills, and much more. These hints will help make your house-training efforts more successful.

Let's Get Physical

There are a number of physical challenges your puppy or dog could face that will affect his housetraining skills. Toy breed puppies, for example, often need to eat several small meals throughout the day to offset potential hypoglycemia; this can upset a housetraining schedule unless those meals are taken into account when creating the schedule.

> ### Step Carefully
> Housetraining is not always a smooth process; you may well hit some rough spots along the way. If you have adopted an older puppy or adult dog with some housetraining issues, the process can be tough. But very, very few dogs are untrainable. These boxes contain information that can help you through those tough times.

Acknowledgments

Thanks to Mary Fish Arango for her wonderful photographs. Mary, you went above and beyond! Thanks!

Trademarks

All terms mentioned in this book that are known to be or are suspected of being trademarks or service marks have been appropriately capitalized. Alpha Books and Penguin Group (USA) Inc. cannot attest to the accuracy of this information. Use of a term in this book should not be regarded as affecting the validity of any trademark or service mark.

A Reliably Housetrained Dog Is a Joy

In This Chapter

- ◆ Understanding housetraining
- ◆ What instinct has to do with it
- ◆ Learning when puppies have to go
- ◆ Setting some realistic housetraining goals

There's nothing more frustrating than climbing out of a warm, comfortable bed and stepping into something damp and disgusting. It gets your day off to a bad start and makes you wonder why you ever agreed to get a dog. Unfortunately, when dogs are not reliably housetrained, their ultimate future is in jeopardy; many will be kicked out of the house and live as backyard dogs while others will be relinquished to the local animal shelter. Very few shelter dogs who are not housetrained are adopted.

Although it often seems to be, housetraining is not a mysterious process known only to dog trainers. Housetraining can and should be an easy training regime built on the dog's natural instincts to keep his bed clean. My youngest dog, Bashir, who is now just 2 years old, went through his entire housetraining process without any accidents in the house at all. No puddles and no piles. Now, I think Bashir is a pretty awesome dog, and I will admit I'm biased. However, your dog can do the same as Bashir; it's not that hard.

Learning All About Housetraining

As a dog trainer, I talk to dog owners every day who are having trouble housetraining their dogs. Often these owners are confused about what, when, and how to housetrain their dogs, and sometimes even about what they want their dogs to do.

Unfortunately, if you don't have a clear understanding of what housetraining is and what your goals are for your dog, you will have a difficult time communicating anything to your dog. And when you and your dog are both confused, well, accidents will continue to happen and frustration and disappointment will build.

My definition of housetraining is simple: it is the process of teaching your puppy or dog to relieve herself when you ask her to do so. Normally she will be asked to do this in a specific spot, but the process also includes learning to relieve herself in different places so that she doesn't have a problem if you're visiting away from home. Housetraining also includes helping the puppy or dog develop bowel and bladder control so she can hold it until it's time for her to go.

Photo by Mary Fish Arango

Dogs who are well trained and reliable are welcome anywhere.

All the Scoop

A dog should never be considered housetrained as long as he's having accidents. There is no such thing as "partially" or "almost" housetrained. With housetraining, it's all or nothing.

A dog who is reliably housetrained is a joy. He is welcome in his own home as well as in the homes of friends and family. He can do therapy dog work in hospitals and schools without worry about an accident. He can travel with you, staying in hotels or friends' homes. On the other hand, the dog who is not house-trained will be left outside, will live his life unwelcome in other places, and could potentially even end up in the local shelter. But before we get into the specifics of how to housetrain your dog, let's take a look at some of the variables that can potentially affect how the process works.

In the Beginning: The Instinct to Keep the Bed Clean

Newborn puppies are helpless. Their eyes and ears are closed, their movements are automatic rather than controlled by conscious design, and they don't do much more than suckle and sleep. They can't even relieve themselves without their mother's help; she licks the puppies' genitals and anus to stimulate them to relieve themselves.

Over the next few weeks the puppies grow stronger. The mother dog continues caring for the puppies, feeding them, keeping them warm, and making sure they relieve themselves. However, at about 5 weeks of age the puppies begin to toddle away from their bed and littermates to relieve themselves. Wise breeders give the puppies a spot where they can go (a sand box, a litter box, or some newspaper) and this can be the first step in housetraining.

This instinct to keep the bed clean is one that has remained through thousands of years of domestication. In the wild, the smell of food in feces could draw additional predators who might kill the puppies. In addition, if the sleeping area is clean, there is less chance of parasites, disease, and vermin. A wild canine who sleeps in a clean bed would potentially live a longer, healthier life.

? All the Scoop

Puppies who have been raised in a cage (such as puppy mill or pet store puppies) are not able to move away from their bed to relieve themselves, and because they have to act against their own instincts, they often have housetraining difficulties later.

By the time the puppies are 7, 8, or 9 weeks of age, most have mastered this lesson. They are aware of their bodies, know when they need to go, and will move away from their bed to do so.

Starting Young

Some puppy owners want to give their puppy some time to adjust to their new home before they begin housetraining. The owners of Tiger, a brindle Mastiff puppy, told me, "He's just a baby! And so cute! We want to just enjoy him right now. We'll start training later."

That's fine if that's what they want to do, but as I explained to them, puppies are genetically programmed to learn at this age. They have no bad habits and are eager little sponges ready to soak up whatever we wish to teach them. Unfortunately, that means they may also learn some things we wish they didn't. If Tiger learns to relieve himself anywhere he wants in the house, his owners may have a hard time changing his mind about that later.

The best time to begin housetraining is when you pull up in front of your house with your new dog. He should immediately (before he is brought into the house) go to the spot where you want him to relieve himself. We'll talk about how to teach him in upcoming chapters, but the idea is that he begins learning the correct process before he makes a mistake.

Teaching the Older Dog

Housetraining a dog who is older than 9 to 14 weeks of age and who has never been housetrained can be a little more difficult, but it's definitely still possible. If you have adopted a new dog or perhaps your dog has some bad housetraining habits, don't give up. You will need to be patient as changing bad habits and learning new ones take time. Just think about how hard it was for you when you tried to change a bad habit; perhaps you tried to eat better or quit smoking. It's tough but you can do it, and it's the same for your dog.

All the Scoop

Most behaviorists (for people and for dogs) agree that it takes from 6 to 8 weeks to fully change a habit, whether it's to change a bad one or begin a new one. So whether you're teaching a baby puppy the basics of housetraining or changing an older dog's bad housetraining habits, it all takes time. Be prepared to be patient.

Although my instructions pertain to housetraining a puppy, follow these instructions anyway for your older dog. If there is anything specific you should do differently for the older dog, I will make note of it. Then, be patient and consistent and the changes in your dog's behavior will happen.

The Differences Between Boys and Girls

While very young, both male and female puppies are easily trained. Although some dog owners swear that males are slower to develop (and build physical self control) than females, an equal number of people say the opposite is true. Having raised a number of puppies of both sexes in a variety of breeds, I can safely say that both sexes are easy to housetrain.

However, once the puppy reaches puberty (any time between 6 and 9 months of age) males can become more difficult. Once a male dog begins lifting his leg to mark things as his own, housetraining can become a whole new game. Neutering the male puppy before he begins lifting his leg will help prevent the problem. Experts state that neutering a male dog will suppress leg lifting behavior in more than 60 percent of male dogs. Making sure he's well trained during puppyhood is obviously the best solution. But if he's been lifting his leg for any period of time (thus building a bad habit), then changing that behavior will require a lot of dedication from you.

Male dogs are not the only ones to lift their legs or mark territory, though. Some female dogs, usually the ones who are quite assertive by temperament, may also lift their leg. I know a female Papillon, Angie, who would lift both back legs at the same time to mark. Her abdomen and back muscles were so strong, she would do this time and again. She wanted the world to know she was the biggest dog around even though she really wasn't! Changing a female leg lifter's opinion about this behavior will take time and patience, just as with a male.

Step Carefully

Dogs do not have to lift their legs to urinate nor must they mark territory. Civilized dogs can be taught that it is a rude and dirty habit. When your young dog first tries to lift his leg, simply interrupt him and walk him away from the vertical object. Tell him to relieve himself away from vertical objects and praise him there. Repeat this whenever he tries to lift his leg. Make sure you praise him when he urinates correctly.

All Breeds Are Not Created Equal

Unfortunately, all dogs and dog breeds are not created equal, especially in regard to housetraining. Some are reputed to have a more difficult time than others.

I have heard many people say toy breeds are slow to housetrain. This could be caused by a couple of different things. First of all, tiny dogs do have a very small bladder. Or it could be that they are so active, they can squat and be away before you even know what's happened. Having owned Papillons for many years in the past, I can say that I found them no more difficult or easy to housetrain than any other breed.

However, and I think this is the telling reason, I have found that because toy breeds are so small, their owners are more likely to put up with the small puddle or pile. With a larger dog, the owner might take the training more seriously. But because cleaning up after the tiny dog is not difficult, the owners don't follow through with the housetraining as well as they could or should, and the toy breeds get the reputation for being difficult.

Let's Get Physical

Most toy breed puppies need to eat three to four tiny meals each day as they can become hypoglycemic (suffer from low blood sugar) if they go too long without eating. These frequent meals require that the puppies relieve themselves more often.

Harder Than Average to Housetrain

There are a few breeds who do have a justified reputation for being slow to housetrain. These breeds might be slow to develop bowel and bladder control, or they might be mentally slow to mature. Some of these include:

- Bichon Frise
- Pugs
- Beagles
- Basset Hounds
- Dachshunds
- Pekingese
- Yorkshire Terriers
- Lhasa Apso
- Chow Chow
- Dalmatian

If you're concerned about this, discuss this issue with a breeder prior to choosing a breed or a puppy.

If you have a breed who is reputed to have difficulty with housetraining or you have a toy breed dog, just follow the directions in this book and be patient. The housetraining will come to these dogs but it might take a little more time.

Gotta Go Now!

Puppies and dogs have some predictable times when they will need to relieve themselves. When you understand these times, you can help make sure your dog relieves herself in the right place.

All puppies are different. Each is an individual and this must be taken into account throughout the housetraining process. But when talking about puppies in general, baby puppies up to about 14 to 16 weeks of age will need to go when they wake up from sleeping, after they have played for a few minutes, and about 10 to 15 minutes after eating. They will also have to go outside about every hour when awake, up to about every hour and a half.

Puppies from 14 weeks to about 20 weeks of age are beginning to develop more bowel and bladder control. They will still need to relieve themselves when they have eaten, after they wake up, and after they have played, but they will be able to control themselves and not go for about 2 to 3 hours if supervised or confined.

Step Carefully

These ages are provided as guidelines so you can see how puppies develop, but don't mark your calendar and expect your puppy to follow these week by week. These are very general, and every puppy is an individual. Your puppy will show you with her actions how she's doing.

After about 5 months of age, the dog gradually grows up, develops more bowel and bladder control, and mentally matures as well. This is a very gradual process, however, moving more quickly with some dogs than with others. Rottweilers, Mastiffs, Great Danes, and Great Pyrenees, for example, are physically very large but are very slow to mature, both mentally and physically. People are more apt to assume the dog is grown up because of her size, when she really is a puppy until 3 to 4 years of age.

The puppy who needs to relieve herself will signal this by sniffing the floor or ground, circling, arching her back, and then assuming the posture to either urinate or defecate. Some puppies create their own behaviors; Bashir likes privacy, so when we're outside and he heads for the bushes, I know he needs to go. The training process will be easier if you learn to read your puppy's actions so you know when something is imminent.

Photo by Mary Fish Arango

Puppies have to relieve themselves after eating, playing, sleeping, and at regular intervals in between.

Establishing Realistic Goals

Before you begin your dog's housetraining, you need to think about your ultimate goal. What do you want this training to teach your dog? Without one or more goals in mind, you may confuse your goal during the initial training.

Do you want your dog to be reliable when he's inside? That means no accidents at all, urine or feces, and that the dog can be trusted whenever he's inside your house and any other building. This should be everyone's goal.

Do you have a back yard? Do you want your dog to eliminate outside? Is there a specific place in the yard where you want him to go? We'll discuss this more in later chapters, especially in regard to choosing the spot, but just think about it right now.

? All the Scoop

Setting goals is very important to the housetraining process, because once you have goals, you can work toward them. If you change your mind or your goals, or change training techniques midway through the training, you and your dog both will be confused and the training will suffer.

Do you live in the city with no yard? Will you need to walk your dog for him to relieve himself? Again, we'll talk about this more in coming chapters, but right now just visualize what would make life easier for your dog and you.

Would you prefer to have your small dog relieve himself in the house? Perhaps in a litter box? Is he small enough to do this and are you willing to clean the box for his lifetime? Once he learns this is the place to go, changing his habits later is tough, so think about this.

Do you have a dog now who has some housetraining issues? What is he doing that you would like to change? Do you want your dog to relieve himself when you tell him to, so that you can travel with him, or make sure he has tried to squeeze out the last drop before bringing him inside?

Once you have decided on some realistic goals, jot them down and post them somewhere you will see them regularly; perhaps on the jar where you keep the dog treats. By reading them often, you can keep them fresh in your mind.

The Least You Need to Know

◆ Housetraining utilizes the puppy's instinct to keep his bed clean.

◆ There can be learning differences between males and females, and various breeds, as well as between puppies and older dogs.

◆ Young puppies need to relieve themselves when they wake up, after eating and playing, and at regular intervals in between.

◆ Having realistic goals can help you keep the training focused.

Teaching Your Dog Is Easy Once You Know How

In This Chapter

- ◆ Understanding how dogs learn
- ◆ Keeping the training positive
- ◆ Avoiding corrections
- ◆ Beginning the training

Puppies begin learning very early in life. One of their first lessons is how hard they can bite. If a puppy bites a littermate too aggressively while playing, his sister or brother will cry, "Yipe!" and the biting puppy will back off. If he bites his mother too hard, perhaps while chewing on her ear in play, she will shake him off and may pin him with a front paw. If he continues to struggle or bites the paw that has him pinned, she will growl at him. In all of these scenarios, he learns that his actions can cause a reaction—a very good first lesson that we will build upon.

We're going to use a training technique that is very easy for most dog owners to understand and implement. At the same time, the dogs are also quick to learn it. This is the same technique that I have used successfully for my last eight or ten dogs, all of whom were successfully housetrained, and the same technique I teach my dog training students.

Most of the examples I use in this chapter pertain to dogs who will have access to a backyard where they can relieve themselves. This is the most common scenario for dogs and owners; however, for those of you who share an apartment or condo with a dog, don't think I've forgotten you. Learn from the examples I give here (because the training techniques still apply), and in future chapters I will discuss specific techniques you can use.

Dogs Are Learning All the Time

Dogs are excellent at training their owners. What? You say your dog hasn't trained you? I bet she has, because most dogs do train their owners. Mine have, although I try to be aware of it. My middle dog, Riker, has a very expressive face and knows that I'm a softie when he opens his eyes wide, tilts his head, and sits nicely in front of me. I am more apt to do what he wants when he does this, and he's learned to use that to his advantage. That's good people training.

When your dog drops her ball in your lap, it's because she's learned that you will throw it for her. When she barks at her leash hanging on the coat rack, she does so because she's learned that's what you hook up to her before you go for a walk. Your dog is learning and teaching all the time.

Our dogs are good trainers because they study us; they watch us and our reactions. They learn what works to their benefit and what doesn't. When we're aware of what they are doing, we can then use it to our advantage. When Riker gives me that puppy look when he wants a treat, I turn it around so he's doing something for me. I'll get him a treat, but before he gets it he has to sit, lie down, come back up to a sit, and then shake hands with me. Then he can have the treat. In other words, I have him work for me first.

Unfortunately, when a dog is good at training his owner and the owner is unaware of what is going on, problems can result. The dog thinks he's in charge because he's making the owner do what he wishes; he thinks he's the leader in the home. Perhaps the dog will begin to growl when someone asks him to get down off the sofa, or he gets a treat every time he begs and then begins to get obese. He may assert himself by lifting his leg on the furniture. It's very important that you pay attention to your dog and watch him, looking for clues of what he does that causes you to respond in some manner. You may find your dog is doing more people training than you would like to admit!

> **Step Carefully**
>
> If your dog growls or snaps at you (or worse yet, bites you) when you ask him to do anything, call your local dog trainer or behaviorist right away. This is serious and you need some help.

You can easily turn the tables on your dog, though, and begin the training so gently your dog doesn't even notice. Dog training doesn't necessarily mean a dog-training class at the park, although most dogs will benefit from such a class. Dog training can be anything where you teach your dog to do something that is good for him or for you, or something that will make your lives together better. Housetraining is definitely one of those things!

Choosing a Command

The very first step in housetraining is choosing a command. You want this word or phrase to mean to your dog, "Try to relieve yourself now." You will use this word or phrase as you teach your puppy what housetraining is, as well as where and when she should try to go.

The word or phrase should be something everyone in the family is willing to say. For example, if you choose "Go tinkle," your husband or teenager may refuse to use the word and may make up their own phrases, which will only confuse the puppy.

All the Scoop

You will be using this phrase for the rest of your dog's life, so although "Go tinkle" might be cute for a fuzzy puppy, it wouldn't quite suit a full-grown Rottweiler or German Shepherd.

Many people use the phrase "Go potty," and that's fine if that is what you wish to say. However, a friend of mine uses the phrase, "Get busy," and I really like that. You can have your dog out in the bushes in public and no one needs to know what you're telling her! It's a great phrase, so good that it's what we're going to use in this book.

You will use this phrase when you take your puppy outside to relieve herself. Wait while she sniffs and finds the right spot. While she's going, tell her quietly, "Get busy!" Your voice needs to be heard but not so much that you interrupt what she's doing. When she's finished, praise her enthusiastically, with your first words being, "Good girl (or boy) to get busy!"

Using Positive Reinforcements

Almost all of us work better when the job we're doing is appreciated. Suppose your boss comes by, pats you on the shoulder, and tells you, "Great job on the last report. It was well done and I appreciate the effort you put into it. Oh, and in thanks there will be a bonus on your next check." You will smile, bask in the glow of his praise, and work even harder on the next project. Why will you work harder? Because we all do better when our efforts are appreciated and rewarded; that's called positive reinforcement.

Your dog is the same way, but positive reinforcements for his housetraining efforts will include your verbal praise, such as "Good boy to get busy!" Positive reinforcements can also include petting, a toss of his favorite ball or toy, or a treat. Notice these are all things dogs usually like; a positive reinforcement doesn't work if the dog (or person) doesn't like the thing being offered. If your boss had offered you a gift card to a restaurant you hate instead of a bonus on your check, your future efforts would probably not be as strong. This means you need to know your puppy. Is he food-motivated? Does he like commercial treats or should you use tiny bits of leftover chicken? Is a tennis ball a better reinforcement than a squeaky toy? Find a few things your puppy really likes and then make sure you have at least one of those things on hand at all times.

> ### Let's Get Physical
> If your dog is chubby and you need to monitor her treat intake or if your dog has some food allergies, use a favorite toy as a positive reinforcement instead of food treats.

You will use these positive reinforcements whenever your puppy does something you want him to do. When he goes outside with you and relieves himself in the correct spot, you will praise him, "Good boy to get busy! Yeah, good job!" as you pet him and give him a treat. After a few repetitions, he will understand that relieving himself in that spot makes you really happy and when you're really happy, good things come his way.

Photo by Mary Fish Arango

Reinforce with positives everything you would like your puppy to do again.

Don't Correct; Don't Punish

In years past, the accepted technique to housetrain a dog was to rub the dog's nose in her accidents. Although some dogs did become trustworthy in the house, I doubt very much that technique had anything to do with it. What this will do, however, is teach a dog to be sneaky.

Urinating and defecating are not problem behaviors. Dogs have to urinate and defecate on a regular basis; these are very normal functions. What can be a problem (to us—not to the dog) is where and when the dog urinates and defecates, and that's what housetraining is all about. If a dog's nose is rubbed in her urine or feces, the dog may begin to think those two substances are the problems. She cannot stop going so she will then try to hide them. She may relieve herself behind the sofa or in a back bedroom. Some dogs get desperate enough that they eat their own feces. The dog will certainly stop relieving herself in your presence, even outside, which will make it harder for you to give her any positive reinforcement when she does do it where she should.

Step Carefully

Corrections and punishments from you that occur after a housetraining accident has already happened do not work. Holding a grudge doesn't work either.

If you do come upon a pile or a puddle, don't yell at your dog, rub her nose in it, hit her with a rolled-up newspaper, or correct her in any way. Instead, simply consider it your mistake. You didn't get her outside soon enough, didn't supervise her well, or failed her in some other aspect of her training. This was your mistake, not hers.

Timing Is Everything

Dogs live in the moment; they don't dwell on the past or worry about the future. Puppies have an even shorter concentration span than adult dogs; their minds flutter about from one thing to another. Trainers must keep this in mind; your timing is very important.

Not only is it vital to get your dog outside when he needs to relieve himself, but your positive reinforcements must be timed correctly, too. For example, let's say you took your puppy outside to relieve himself. He's sniffing the ground, getting ready to go, but instead of watching him, you get distracted and begin pinching off the rose blossoms that have gone by on your rose bushes. The puppy relieves himself while you weren't paying attention, and wanders over to you. You realize he's done and praise him, "Good boy to get busy!"

It's too late. He's thinking of something else already. Perhaps he smells the roses you have pinched off, or he's sniffing the grass at your feet. You can praise him but it won't mean anything to him and you've lost that opportunity to reinforce his good behavior.

This timing is important in the house, too. Let's say your puppy is in the family room with you. You see him begin to sniff the carpet and your mind says, "Ah ha! In the book, Liz said puppies sniff the floor before they go!" and you grab up puppy, take him outside, place him in his spot and tell him, "Puppers, get busy!" That's good timing. You didn't scold him, you prevented an accident from occurring, got him outside, and now have a chance to praise him when he does it in the right spot.

Cleanliness Is Imperative

Have you ever walked past a fire hydrant, got a whiff of something horrible, and grimaced as you went on past it? I often feel sorry for the firefighters who need to work with that hydrant! Male (and some dominant female) dogs mark upright objects (including fire hydrants) as a means of saying, "I was here!" As each dominant dog walks by, he (or she) will mark that same spot.

When my youngest dog, Bashir, was a puppy, we went for a walk down at our local boat harbor. It's a favorite place for people to walk their dogs. Obviously one particular fire hydrant was the most important hydrant in the place because it smelled— even to me—and Bashir walked around way out to the end of his leash. He wanted nothing to do with that!

If you have several dogs and one (or more) is a leg lifter, you can have a game of one-upmanship, with each dog marking over the other dogs' markings. If you just have one dog but he's marking his territory in the house, it could be because he sees another dog outside, hears a neighbor's dog barking, or he's simply trying to make sure everyone understands this is his house. No matter why he's doing it, it's bad behavior.

Step Carefully

If you think you have two leg lifters, you will have to separate the two so you can find out which dog is marking inside. Once you know whether one (or both) is causing the problem, then you can begin training.

Leg lifters are not the only dogs to keep hitting the same spot, though. Most dogs will return to the same spot on the floor or carpet or on the grass outside to relieve themselves. Not only are dogs creatures of habit, but they can also smell where urine has been deposited previously. Carpet is especially bad because the urine may have soaked through to the carpet padding. That means your cleaning efforts must be very thorough so you can get rid of any lingering scent.

The best products to clean up after dog accidents are those made specifically for this. These products contain enzymes that continue to work in the fabric or carpet, digesting the remaining urine or feces. You can find these products at pet-supply stores, on pet-supply websites, or in pet-supply catalogs (see Appendix A). Do not use ammonia-based cleaners; those smell like urine to your dog and will draw him right back to the same spot.

If your dog has been having a number of accidents in the house, either on carpet or on furniture, you may want to invest in an inexpensive black light. Black lights highlight urine stains, even those you cannot see. Wait until evening, close all the drapes, turn off all the lights, and turn on the black light. Have some enzyme cleaner at hand and begin scrubbing.

If you have just moved into a new (to you) home and your dog has been having accidents, pick up one of these black lights. The dog belonging to the previous resident may have had accidents in the house and your dog is reacting to the stranger's scent.

Limiting Your Dog's Freedom

Preventing accidents from happening is a huge part of housetraining. Dogs return to the same spot (or spots) time after time. As you now know, correcting the dog when you find a puddle or pile will not work (will not teach the dog what to do), so you need to prevent accidents from occurring while you teach her where she's supposed to go to relieve herself.

All the Scoop

Remember, this training is focused on teaching your dog what to do, where to do it, and when. It is not directed at what not to do because dogs have to relieve themselves.

Indoors

Puppies are born with the instinct to keep their bed clean and to move away from it to relieve themselves, but they will not regard your entire house as a bed. The puppy's crate is his bed, or perhaps even the room where his crate is located. But the rest of the house will be 'other than bed' and therefore, free to be a toilet.

Therefore, your dog should be in the room with you rather than roaming the house unsupervised. If it's a relatively small room where you can see the puppy at all times, she can have free run of that room. If it's a large room or a room with large pieces of furniture where the puppy can sneak away, then have her on leash and keep her close to you.

Close the door to the room so the puppy can't wander away, or put up a baby gate across the doorways or hallways. You want to make sure the puppy cannot wander away from you. If you cannot supervise the puppy at all, put her in her crate (we'll discuss crate training in the next chapter) or in a safe place outside in the yard.

Untrained dogs who have free run of the house can get into way too much trouble, and unless you catch them in the act, there is nothing you can do about it later. They can have housetraining accidents, chew on electrical cords, destroy the television remote, raid the trash cans, and so much more. I do not allow my dogs free, unsupervised run of the house until they are at least 2 years of age—once they have proven to me that they are mature enough to handle the responsibility.

Photo by Mary Fish Arango

Freedom is not a right; it is earned with good behavior and mental maturity.

Although punishment—rubbing the dog's nose in his mess, yelling screaming, and hitting with rolled up newspapers—has long been a part of dog training; it has no place here. These training techniques cause too much anxiety, can potentially damage your relationship with your dog, and have no bearing whatsoever on housetraining. When we look back on the training techniques of years past, it's actually amazing that dogs' learned as much as they did!

Outside

Your dog should be on leash outside, too. If you have a fenced-in, secure backyard, that doesn't mean your dog should have free run of it, especially during housetraining lessons. When you take your dog outside to relieve himself, take him out on leash so you can bring him to the spot where you wish him to go. Then you can tell him what to do and then praise him when he does it.

If he's not on leash, he may decide to play instead of concentrating on what he should do. Or worse yet, he may decide to relieve himself in the flower or vegetable garden. Without a leash, it is difficult, if not impossible to control and teach him.

After he has relieved himself, then take the leash off and he can have some freedom to run and play. He needs the exercise and you both will benefit from one or two play sessions each day.

Leash Training

As I just mentioned, your dog should be on leash when you take him to relieve himself so that you have a little control over his actions. The leash training your dog needs to know for housetraining is very basic. Don't worry about his pulling or having him heel; instead, all your dog needs to do is be able to walk on the leash without fighting it or planting himself like a stone. Later you can teach him better leash skills for your walks together.

All the Scoop

For this training, the leash should be connected to the dog's buckle collar—the one she wears all the time that has her identification tags on it. There is no need for a special training collar or head halter.

If you have a very young puppy or a dog who has never been leash trained, keep the initial training sessions very short and positive. Hook the leash up to your dog's collar just prior to feeding him. Let the leash drag and let him feel it pull from its own weight. Feed him and have him wear it for just a couple of minutes after he's eaten. Take it off him before you pick him up to take him outside to relieve himself. (Remember, he has to go after he's eaten!)

When he's comfortable having the leash on during meals, let him drag it around the house when he's in the room with you. Watch to make sure the leash doesn't get tangled, but otherwise let him drag it, step on it, and get used to the feel of it on his neck.

After a few sessions of that, you can teach him to follow you. Have some really good treats in one hand while you have the leash in the other. Let your puppy smell the treats, and slowly back away from him as you say, "Puppers, follow me! Good!" Continue to encourage him; then when he's taken a few steps toward you, give him the treat. And then repeat the exercise.

You will find your dog catches on to this very quickly, and when he does, continue using the treat as a lure but begin walking forward together. Again, encourage him and give him the treat after a few steps. Gradually increase the number of steps until the both of you can walk across the room, out the door, and to his potty area.

Asking to Go Outside

Later, when your dog is well housetrained, you will want her to have a way to tell you when she needs to go outside. Just as most dogs are very good at training their owners, most also figure out how to get your attention. My three dogs each has his or her own way to tell me they need to go out. Dax, my oldest, finds me and then stares at me. She positions herself so she can stare at my face and then does so until I look at her. I know what the stare means, so when I see her do this, I ask, "Do you have to go outside?" and she will dash toward the door.

Step Carefully

I use two different phrases for two different things. "Do you have to go outside?" means exactly that; it does not necessarily mean that the dog needs to relieve himself. "Get busy" means "Try to relieve yourself right now." When you are asking the dog to go outside, do not tell him to relieve himself. After all, you don't want him to do it in the doorway!

The two boys, on the other hand, are much more active. Riker nudges my arm with his nose, and if that doesn't work, he shoves his head under my arm. Bashir dances around until I pay attention to him. Both boys, like Dax, dash to the door when I respond to their communication efforts. And, of course, I always praise them for telling me.

The start of these communication efforts begins right now, in the beginning of the housetraining. When your puppy or dog is walking nicely on the leash so you can walk her to the door to go outside rather than picking her up and carrying her, begin asking her, "Do you have to go outside? Huh? Do you?" in a happy, playful tone of voice. Your dog is going to respond to that voice happily and most likely will wag her tail, wiggle, or dance.

Begin this conversation in various rooms of the house; don't wait until right before you get to the back door. When you begin in various rooms of the house, your dog will learn she can begin to communicate with you there. If you wait until you get to the back door, you will end up with a dog dancing at the back door to go outside rather than a dog who will go look for you.

In and Out Doggy Doors

Doggy doors have some very real benefits, especially for dog owners who are away from the house for hours at a time. However, giving the dog, especially an untrained dog or young puppy, unlimited access to the house is not a good idea. Too much freedom can lead to other behavior problems, including destructive chewing, trash can raiding, and numerous other puppy problems. There's a balance that must be reached; he needs access to the backyard, security, and shelter, but you also need to prevent him from getting into trouble and learning bad habits.

The ideal location for a doggy door is where the dog can gain access to shelter from the weather but will not be in an area of the house where he can cause damage while unsupervised. If the doggy door opens into the laundry room or garage, or even to an area of the kitchen, that will work. This area can then be portioned off using a movable fence, such as an exercise pen or sections of lattice. In this area the dog can have a bed or some old towels, some chew toys, and a bowl of water.

Outside, the doggy door can lead to an area of the yard that is secure and safe. A dog run is great for this or a fenced-off section of the yard.

All the Scoop

A doggy door should never replace the regular housetraining. Your dog still needs to learn where to go, when to go, and how to tell you she needs to go.

To teach your dog to go in and out of the doggy door, you'll need another family member to help you. Both of you should have some really good dog treats (like diced chicken or cheese). One of you will be inside the house at the doggy door while the other person will be outside. The person with the dog will hold the dog at the doggy door, while the person outside lifts the flap so he can see the dog, shows the dog the treat, and calls him through. When the dog comes through, he gets praised enthusiastically and gets a treat. Then repeat the exercise, calling the dog back inside.

When the dog will come through easily, repeat the exercise, lifting the flap about halfway open. When the dog can do that well and with confidence, then just touch the flap enough to get it moving and send the dog through. You may have to repeat this entire training session several times over several days before your dog is bold enough to go through it without your encouragement.

The Least You Need to Know

- ◆ Choose a command that you will be able to use throughout the dog's lifetime, even out in public.

- ◆ Use positive reinforcements to reward the dog's cooperation.

- ◆ Never scold or punish the dog if you find an accident.

- ◆ Teach your dog to tell you that she needs to go outside.

Introducing Crate Training

In This Chapter

- ◆ Understanding why dog crates work
- ◆ Choosing the right crate
- ◆ Introducing the crate to your dog
- ◆ Using it wisely

As I am sitting at my computer writing this book, my middle dog, Riker, is curled up under the desk at my feet. He enjoys cavelike places. His enjoyment is not rooted in any insecurities or fears; this is a dog I have had since he was 9 weeks old. He is confidant, intelligent, bold, and very secure in his place in my home and heart.

Wild canines (wolves, coyotes, foxes, and feral dogs) all like dens. Dens provide security from outside threats and give the canine a place where she can relax, sleep, and raise pups. Our dogs still have those instincts. That's why Riker is under my desk and why so many dogs curl up under the foot of the recliner or sleep under the coffee table. Using a crate to housetrain puppies utilizes this natural instinct to have a safe place to sleep.

What Is a Crate?

Commercial crates were originally designed for shipping animals. If you watch any of the zoo shows on the animal channels on television, you can see everything from condors to meerkats to wolves being transported in plastic, boxlike containers. About 25 years ago, these crates began gaining popularity as tools for preventing bad behaviors in dogs. Previously most dogs learned their house-training skills in a haphazard manner, often by being relegated to the backyard for hours at a time. But the crate utilized the dog's instinct to keep his bed clean, and housetraining became much easier.

All the Scoop

I would love to give credit where credit is due and acknowledge the person who introduced crate training to mainstream trainers and dog owners, but in all my research, I have yet to find out who that person is. But to that mystery person I say, "Thank you!"

Today, crate training is a widely accepted training tool. It can help with housetraining, it can keep puppies and untrained dogs safe, and it can help prevent problem behaviors. However, as with all training tools, it can also be abused. So in this chapter, as well as showing you how to use the crate, I will also give you guidelines so you don't unintentionally misuse the crate.

Taking a Look at the Types of Crates

Although many years ago the only types of crates available were the boxlike plastic ones, today there are a number of different brands and types of crates to choose from. The original plastic crate has a top piece and bottom piece that are held together with bolts that can be tightened and loosened by hand, and a grill door. These crates have solid sides with air holes or vents. The solidity of these crates creates a denlike feel and so provides the dog with security. They are sturdy and many brands are approved by the airlines for airplane travel. Unfortunately, even though the top and bottom come apart, they can still be quite bulky.

There are a couple of brands of plastic crates that come in several pieces, making them more portable. These are not approved for airline travel but can be quite convenient if your dog might travel by car with you. Their portability can also make them easier to move around the house.

Let's Get Physical

When riding in the car, one of the safest places for your dog to ride is in his crate, which is held in place with a seat belt. If you must brake hard, or swerve, or worse yet, are involved in an accident, he is restrained.

Wire crates are made from heavy gauge wire and are more cagelike than the plastic crates. These are great for dogs who need more ventilation (dogs with short muzzles, such as Pugs and Pekingese) or dogs living in a hot, humid climate. However, because the crate has open bars, it doesn't give the dog the sense of security that enclosed crates provide. Although these crates usually fold up so they can be transported, they are often quite heavy, especially the larger sizes. These crates are very good for dogs who like to chew, though, and are sturdier than the plastic crates.

In recent years, several different manufacturers have come out with soft-sided crates. These have been made from canvas or other tough materials that are supposed to hold up under the wear and tear of housing a dog. Ventilation is usually provided by screens on the sides and the door. Because they have soft sides, these crates fold or roll up so storage is much easier than with the rigid crates. Because of their portability, many dog-show and performance-event attendees use these for their dogs. However, these crates should not be used with puppies, dogs in training, or dogs who are "escape artists." Many dogs have chewed or torn their way out of these crates, often quite quickly.

There is no one crate type that is correct for every dog owner, dog, and situation. So look around. Check out your local pet stores and super-discount stores. Lift each of the crates, check out their sturdiness, weight, and portability. Open and close the door. If they are supposed to fold up, do that, and then set it back up again. Think about your individual dog, your household, and how you would use

the crate. Then choose the right style for you and
your dog.

Photo by Mary Fish Arango

*There are several different types of crates and
each has its good points and bad.*

Choosing the Right Size

The fit of the crate to your dog is just as important
as her collar fit is. If the collar is too small, your
dog will choke and be uncomfortable; yet if the
collar is too big, she can slip out of it and perhaps
become lost.

Crates that are too small will cause your dog to be curled up, uncomfortable, and stiff. She could also potentially overheat in a too-small crate. If the crate is too big for your puppy, she could relieve herself in a corner of the crate and still have room to move away from her mess.

The ideal crate will enable your dog room to stand up without hitting her head on the top, and have room to lie down comfortably, with room to shift and change position. This means her needs will change as she grows.

> **Step Carefully**
>
> You may be able to find a used crate at a flea market or garage sale for much less than you would have to spend elsewhere. If the crate is intact and in good condition, just make sure you take it apart and thoroughly clean it with a diluted bleach solution (a cup of household bleach to 1 gallon of hot water) prior to using it for your dog.

You can handle this several different ways. If you plan on adding another dog to your family in a few years, you may want to have crates of several sizes. My husband and I do this. We have a puppy-sized crate, an adult-sized crate, and two in-between sizes. When a size isn't needed, it's taken apart, cleaned, and stored in the garage rafters where it's out of the way. The crates can be used over and over again for various dogs.

You may also want to simply invest in a crate that will suit your dog when she's full-grown. You will then want to create a divider that will section off the crate so that you can gradually give the puppy more room as she grows. Although some experts recommend using cardboard to create this divider, I have found that too many puppies enjoy chewing and tearing up cardboard, thereby creating a potentially bad habit.

Instead, if you or someone you know is handy with tools, a sturdy plastic divider works better. The divider should be able to fit into the crate snugly so the puppy can't knock it down. A few crate manufacturers have recognized this need and now produce these dividers, sparing dog owners the difficulty of doing this themselves. You may be able to find these at your local pet-supply store; however, not all of the manufacturers have produced these dividers, so if you can't find one, you can make one yourself.

One, Two, or Three?

When you're planning on how you are going to use the crate, think about your daily routine and lifestyle, because this affects where the crate should be located and how many crates you may want to have. For example, ideally, the dog should sleep in someone's bedroom (I'll talk about that in the next section). But during the day you don't want your puppy to be isolated should he need to be crated; he needs to be near the family. Plus, he should go places with you in the car.

If the crate is lightweight and easily portable, you can get by with one and just move it around. However, if you have a heavy, sturdy crate or a big dog, it might not be as easy to move the crate.

All the Scoop

The crate is not just for use during puppyhood or the housetraining process; instead, it should be used throughout puppyhood and adolescence and on into young adulthood when most dogs tend to get into trouble. When your dog is mentally grown up (2 to 3 years old) then you can take the door off and the crate is simply your dog's bed and place of refuge.

So think about an investment in more than one crate. And they are an investment; they're an investment in your dog's safety, his future good behavior, and his place in the family.

Choosing the Right Location

Ideally, your puppy should sleep in the bedroom with you so you can hear him fidget should he need to go outside during the night. This also gives the puppy time to be with you; he gets 8 hours of smelling you and hearing you breathe. That's time with you he might otherwise not have. If space is limited and he has a big crate, put it next to your bed in place of the nightstand. It's not fancy furniture but it works.

During the day when you're home with the puppy, you might want to have another crate in a more central location where he can be with the family, yet confined when no one can supervise him. The crate can be in the family room or living room—anywhere people normally gather. When I have a puppy at home, I have a second crate here in my office so the puppy can be with me during the day, yet I can concentrate on work and don't have to worry about the puppy wandering off and getting in trouble.

Introducing the Crate

Because your dog will be using this crate for many years, the introduction is very important. Your dog should look upon the crate as her bed as well as her place of safety and security. Of course, that means you should have a positive outlook toward the crate, too, because if you think it's a doggy jail, your dog will pick up on your feelings.

To introduce your puppy to the crate, open the crate door and block it so it cannot swing shut. Have one of your puppy's favorite toys (tennis ball, squeaky toy, or rope toy) and toss it toward (but not inside) the crate. Encourage her to get the toy as you normally do during play. Repeat the game by tossing the toy all around the outside of the crate, front, back, and sides, even to the point of bouncing the toy off the side of the crate. Stop after 6 to 8 throws, take your puppy outside to relieve herself (she has to go after playing), and then give her a break.

All the Scoop

If your puppy doesn't have a favorite toy or won't chase after one, then use tiny bits of treats instead.

In an hour or so, repeat the same exercise, except that after three or four throws, begin tossing the toy (or treat) inside the crate. Tell your puppy when she goes inside for the toy, "Sweetie, kennel!" and then praise her, making sure to praise her when she is inside the crate. Timing is important; tell her to kennel as she is going into the kennel and praise her for being inside the crate—not for leaving the crate! When she has gone inside several times, stop, take her outside again (because puppies have to relieve themselves after activity), and give her a chance to relax.

For your next crate-training session, take a handful of her puppy-food kibbles or a few small treats and toss them into the crate. When she goes in to eat them, close the door behind her. Give her a chance to discover the door is closed, praise her, and wait 5 seconds, then open the door. Repeat this a few more times, gradually increasing the time while making sure to open the door only when the puppy is quiet. Never open the door when she's throwing a temper tantrum or barking.

At this point in the introduction, begin feeding your puppy in her crate. Place the food bowl in the back of the crate and let the puppy go in after it as you tell her, "Sweetie, kennel." The food can serve as the reward. The first time or two you do this, don't close the door after her. Let her go in and out as she pleases. But the third time, close the door after her. When she's finished eating, turns around and discovers the door is closed, wait a few seconds before you open the door. Gradually, over the next few meals, increase the time before you open the door.

Most puppies accept the crate very quickly after these few daily training sessions. A few puppies are resistant but with some meals, toys, treats, and praise, even they will accept it. After all, puppies are not far removed from being in a den (or whelping box) with their mother.

Photo by Mary Fish Arango

Introduce the crate gradually so your dog learns that it is a good thing.

However, sometimes an adult dog being introduced to the crate will fight it—barking, crying, biting the door, and throwing herself around. It is vitally important that you never open the crate door when the dog is behaving badly; that rewards the bad behavior. By opening the door then, the dog learns that acting horribly causes the door to open, and that is not the message you want her to learn.

For it to be effective, the crate should be one your dog will like, because you are going to use it until your dog is grown up, well trained, and has no behavior problems in the house. And even then you may take the door off it and let it serve as your dog's bed. In addition, you may need a crate in the car or during travel. So make sure you introduce the crate gradually. Make sure your timing is good and that you're praising the dog when she's going in the crate and is inside; don't praise her as she leaves the crate.

Using the Crate Correctly

The instinct that puppies have to keep their bed clean will work during crate training as long as the puppy is not confined too long. Most 8- to 10-week-old puppies can sleep through the night with only one trip outside, and many can make it all night (6 hours more or less) by 12 weeks of age. But that's not set in stone; every puppy is different. During the day, puppies will have to go outside much more often and will always have to go out after eating, drinking, playing, and when waking up from a nap.

Let's Get Physical

If, during crate training or housetraining, your puppy's schedule changes drastically and he begins urinating or defecating more than he has previously, get him to the veterinarian as there may be a physical cause for the change in routine.

If your dog needs to be in the crate for a few hours during the day, give him one of the toys available now that dispenses food or treats. There are several on the market and most are very good; just choose one that your dog cannot destroy. Put some treats or dry kibbled dog food inside it and give it to your dog when you put him in the crate. This will reward him for going into the crate and at the same time keep him amused. In addition, by the time he gets all the food out, he'll be ready for a nap.

You will have to let your dog out of the crate when he needs to relieve himself, so it's important you know when he's fussing to go outside. Many dogs will get restless, move around, whine a bit, and then if you haven't responded, they will bark. This bark is usually different from the dog's bark that says he's upset because he's crated, so it's important you know his vocabulary. If you let him out because you think he needs to relieve himself, and when you take him outside, he doesn't go, then bring him in and put him back in the crate. Do not reward him for barking just because he's bored.

How Long Is Too Long?

Puppies and dogs being housetrained should spend the night in the crate. This isn't the time to let the dog climb into bed with you or sleep on the floor in the bedroom; instead, the dog should sleep in the crate and develop the bowel and bladder control needed to make it through the night. It can take several months to develop this kind of control, though, so be patient.

During the day, young puppies may be crated for an hour at a time here and there throughout the day, but as a general rule should not spend more than 4 hours total in the crate. Puppies this age need time to run and play, socialize with people and other dogs, and explore the world around them. In addition, if crated too many hours during the day, the puppy won't want to sleep at night.

Step Carefully

If you work during the day or are away from home for hours at a time, you may need to be creative so that the puppy isn't crated for too many hours at a stretch. If you have a backyard, you may want to build a safe dog run, or you can hire a dog walker or neighbor to come take your puppy out at regular intervals.

Older dogs can spend more time in the crate once they've developed control, but again, don't leave the dog crated all day and then crate him again all night. That's a misuse of the crate.

The Crate Should Never Be Used as Punishment

If you walk into the living room and see a puddle on the floor or a chewed-up shoe, don't drag the puppy to his crate and toss him in as you scold him. Don't stand outside the crate and yell at your dog, even if he's been fussing and whining. If you have lost your patience for any reason (raising a dog can be tough sometimes), don't toss the dog into the crate and then slam the door behind him. The crate should never be used as punishment.

Our entire approach on crate training is focused on using the dog's natural instincts to want a clean den; if the crate is used as punishment, the dog will resist going into it, and once in, will whine, cry, or bark to get back out. Once the dog is afraid of the crate or dislikes it, it's tough to change his mind. However, if you've already reached this point and need to change his mind, the easiest way is to invest in a different type of crate (if you were using plastic, get a wire one) and start the training all over from the beginning.

Time-Out Is Okay

While the crate should never be used as punishment, it is perfectly acceptable to use it as a place for a time-out. The difference between a time-out and a punishment is your attitude and bearing. For example, in the last section, I said that you shouldn't toss the dog in the crate and slam the door, nor should you stand outside the crate yelling.

Those actions and others that the dog would consider punishments are very negative and will cause the dog to dislike the crate.

However, if your dog gets overly excited during playtimes in the house and doesn't want to calm down, you can take his collar and calmly walk him to his crate, put him inside, and leave him there for 15 or 20 minutes. This time out in the crate will give him a chance to calm down. There is no yelling, no fighting, no slamming of the crate door; all is calm.

All the Scoop

The time-out in the crate can be compared to sitting a child in a chair for a few minutes to calm down; in a time-out, both dog and child get a chance to take a few deep breaths and relax.

Don't use time-outs as an excuse to leave the dog in the crate too much, though. The dog should still, even with time-outs, never be left in the crate during the day for more than 4 hours. If overused, time-outs will lose their effectiveness.

The Least You Need to Know

◆ Using a crate for training utilizes the dog's natural denning instincts and desire to keep her bed clean.

◆ The crate should be introduced gradually with verbal praise, treats, and toys as reinforcements.

◆ Dogs can spend the night in the crate but then should only spend up to 4 hours in it during the day.

◆ Never use the crate for punishment; that will cause the dog to dislike the crate.

Health Problems Can Sabotage Housetraining

In This Chapter

- ◆ Understanding digestion
- ◆ Feeding the best foods
- ◆ Water is necessary for good health
- ◆ When to call the veterinarian

A part of the housetraining process is controlling urination and defecation—basically where and when your dog performs those natural acts. To be able to put any kind of control over those acts, you also need to know how they happen and what can affect them. What, when, and even where your dog eats and drinks has a huge impact on when and even what he eliminates later. If your dog loves water, plays in the swimming pool, and during his play swallows a lot of water, well, then he's going to need to get outside to urinate many times over the next few hours.

There are other factors that can affect your house-training efforts, including veterinary problems. Some young puppies develop urinary tract infections and will urinate every 10 minutes because they feel uncomfortable. Medications can cause house-training difficulties, too. But when you understand all the variables, you can then continue to set your dog up to succeed in his housetraining efforts.

The Mysteries of Digestion

Many people find their own digestive system to be very mysterious, so understanding their dog's is impossible. However, to really comprehend the housetraining process, you should have a basic understanding of how your dog metabolizes his food.

The digestive process in humans begins when food is first eaten. Humans' salivary glands produce saliva, which contains digestive enzymes; these are mixed with the food during chewing. So by the time a person's food is swallowed, digestion has already begun. The dog's saliva, however, is primarily a lubricant to aid in the swallowing of the food. The saliva does not begin the digestive process.

All the Scoop

Dogs don't chew their food. Their jaws move only up and down, with no sideways motion. Dogs bite and tear their food, and will crunch it two or three times so that it becomes small enough to swallow, but proportionately, it is not nearly as small as our food is when we swallow.

When the food is swallowed, it goes to the stomach, which churns the food and mixes it with gastric acids. In humans, this is a continuation of the digestive process, while in dogs it is the first step.

The primary digestion occurs in the small intestine (both for people and dogs). There the food is mixed with bile, pancreatic enzymes, and other digestive enzymes. As the food is broken down into its chemical parts, those chemical parts are absorbed through the walls of the small intestine where they are passed into the circulatory system and then into the individual cells. In the large intestine, water and some remaining chemical electrolytes in the water are absorbed through the intestinal walls. By the time the food reaches the rectum, it is a fairly solid mass of waste.

Although there are several small differences in digestion between humans and canines, the primary one is that dogs lack the digestive enzyme amylase, which digests starches. Because of this lack, many carbohydrates (starches) in the dog's food are eliminated undigested along with the dog's wastes.

Feeding Your Dog

There are hundreds of commercial dog foods being produced today. There are dry dog foods, canned, and semi-moist foods, as well as cooked or raw frozen foods and even dehydrated dog foods. These foods vary from junk food for dogs to well-researched and tested, excellent diets. So what should your dog eat? It would take a book twice the size of this one to discuss all of the important aspects of canine nutrition, so I will just touch briefly on the aspects that pertain to basic health and housetraining.

Very simply, just keep in mind that what goes into your dog must in turn come out.

If your dog is eating a good-quality food of ingredients she can easily digest, then her feces should be formed, firm, and relatively small. She will defecate once or twice a day.

If she's eating a poor-quality food with a lot of fillers and fiber, her stools will be large, will smell, and may be soft. She will defecate three to four times per day.

If the feces are soft and smell bad (out-of-the-ordinary bad) that usually means she has eaten something that has upset her digestive system; perhaps ingredients she can't digest, or the food is too high in fat, or she's raided the garbage can. She may defecate several times each day.

If the dog has a lot of flatulence, the food may be too high in undigestible carbohydrates. She may defecate several times each day.

A dog eating a diet too high in fats may not only gain weight but may have soft stools while a dog not getting enough fat may have dry skin. There are so many variables, it can be confusing to try to find the right food for your dog.

> **? All the Scoop**
> Foods too high in carbohydrates,
> especially cereal grains, can also
> cause a type of hyperactivity in dogs,
> especially in puppies. Dog trainers see it all
> the time; the puppies simply cannot sit still
> and they have a hard time concentrating
> on any training. Changed to a diet higher
> in animal protein, with carbohydrates from
> sources other than cereal grains, the dog
> calms down significantly.

Selecting the Right Food

Dog food is one of those areas when the adage,
"You get what you pay for," usually does apply. For
the most part, the dog foods that cost the least are
usually made with cheaper ingredients, primarily
leftover meat pieces and lots of inexpensive cereal
grains. The more expensive dog foods usually contain the better-quality ingredients. I say "usually"
because that's not always the case.

The pet food recalls of 2007 taught us that many of
the so-called better brand foods (the more expensive brands) were being made at the same plants
where the lower priced foods were produced. We
also found out that many of these foods had the
same sources for ingredients. These recalls were an
eye-opener for many people; experts as well as pet
owners.

To try and keep your pet safe, one of the most important things you should do when evaluating your dog's food is read the label. Don't rely entirely on the food's price, or on advertising or a well-laid-out graphic design; look at what is actually in the food. The first ingredient should be a meat, and it should simply state the type of meat, such as chicken, turkey, or beef. If it says meat and bone meal, or meat by-products, then that food contains the lesser cuts of meats and not the better-quality muscle meats.

The better-quality foods provide carbohydrates from foods more naturally eaten by canines, such as some fruits, tubers, and vegetables. Many wild canines will dig up tubers and eat fallen fruits, but not a one has ever boiled a pot of rice. Keep in mind, dogs do not digest cereal grains well, and many grains, like corn, will pass through undigested.

Avoid also the lesser quality parts of the cereal grains; such as the glutens or middlings. Do not feed your dog wheat middlings or wheat gluten, nor corn gluten or rice gluten. These are in the food to make it stick together and to boost the protein count. Many dogs react badly to glutens and your dog is better nourished by getting his protein from meat.

When you read the label, make sure you understand what the ingredients are. If there are a lot of chemical names, those might be synthetic vitamins, but look them up to make sure. Look up any preservatives, too, to verify they are safe.

Let's Get Physical

What your dog eats affects more than his stools; his health depends upon a good-quality food. A dog eating a poor food may have a dull coat, dry or flakey skin, poor energy levels, and decreased stamina. His immune system and his ability to heal will be affected. He will have a poor attention span and may have trouble learning. Eventually it can also lead to disease and a shortened life span.

The subject of dog foods is one of those areas where everyone disagrees with everyone else. One expert may say that dry, kibbled dog foods are excellent nutrition while another will stress the importance of a more natural diet made up of raw meats. While research on your part is always a good idea, you should also go with what feels right to you and what works for your dog. If you feel uncomfortable preparing raw meat for your dog, he's thriving on a dry dog-food diet, and your veterinarian is comfortable with what your dog is eating, well, then that's fine. A healthy dog on a good diet will show it; he will be bright eyed, alert, quick to work and play, with energy to spare and a shiny coat.

Changing Foods

If you decide to change your dog's food, do so gradually. Your dog's system is adjusted to his old food and anything new can cause an upset. You may have noticed a change even if your dog gets too many treats one day; that night or the next morning, his stools may be soft or just different.

Begin the change by adding one third of the new food to two thirds of the dog's old food. If the dog is tolerating that well with no soft stools, then continue for a week just like that. If he has soft stools, though, decrease the change slightly to one quarter the new food and three quarters the old food. Over a 3-week period, gradually increase the rate of change until by the beginning of the fourth week the dog is eating the new food all by itself.

If the food change is very drastic, such as from a dry kibble food to a raw food diet, or to a dehydrated food, expect a little digestive upset. You can ease this by making the change slowly and by adding some yogurt to your dog's food. The yogurt should have the live active cultures (probiotics) that help balance the digestive system. (The packaging will say "Live active cultures.") A small dog could have a teaspoon while a large dog should get a full tablespoon.

Setting up Mealtimes

Dogs have to relieve themselves after they have eaten. Adults dogs may need to go outside a half an hour or so after eating, but many puppies will need to go outside almost immediately. This is another instance where it's important to pay attention to your dog so you know what's normal, what to expect, and when to be ready to get your dog outside.

*What your dog eats is important, both to her
good health and to her behavior.*

To aid in housetraining, it's important to have
scheduled mealtimes. When meals arrive on time,
every day, housetraining is then that much easier
because the dog's system is on a regular routine.
Dogs are also creatures of habit; they thrive on a
routine.

Baby puppies up to about 12 weeks of age usually
need to eat three times a day. When those times are
will depend on your schedule and the routine you
establish with your dog, but ideally, those mealtimes

should be spread out evenly throughout the time the dog is awake during the day.

> **Let's Get Physical**
>
> Toy breed puppies should eat at least twice a day as their small size makes them more prone to hypoglycemia (low blood sugar). Talk to your veterinarian if you have any questions or concerns.

By 4 months of age most dogs can go to two meals a day, and often by 6 to 7 months of age, many dogs stop eating one of their meals or show less interest in one. Although many breeders and veterinarians recommend two meals a day, many dogs just don't eat that often. When you consider in the wild most canines have a feast-or-famine type of lifestyle (they gorge when they have a meal and then fast until the next meal comes along), you can see where two small meals may not be as natural as one large meal. So set up your dog's mealtimes so they work for you, your schedule, and your dog's natural biorhythms.

Don't Leave Food Out All the Time

If you noticed in the previous section, I mentioned food in terms of mealtimes. There was nothing said about leaving food out all the time because I don't want you to do that. Free feeding, as it's called, creates several different problems, including difficulties with housetraining.

When food is out all the time, your dog is going to munch a little here and nibble a little there instead of eating a meal. When is he going to need to go outside? You know he needs to go out after he's eaten a full meal, but if he's munching, it's impossible to predict. That makes housetraining significantly harder.

If, at some point, your dog doesn't feel good, one of the first questions your veterinarian is going to ask is, "How's his appetite?" If your dog free feeds, that question will be tough to answer.

Dog trainers like myself tend to look at food in another way. I feel it's important your dog understands that his food comes from you, his adoptive parent and leader, so when you feed him scheduled meals you are handing him the food he then eats. Amazingly enough this is important; to a dog, the giver of the food is very significant. I even like to suggest that the owners of newly adopted dogs hand-feed a part of each meal—especially if their dogs are worried or afraid. By getting their food from your hand, they can then more quickly bond with you and learn to trust you.

Water Is Life

The adult dog's body is between 65 and 80 percent water, depending upon the dog's age, breed, and size. Water is essential to the chemistry of life and is in almost every cell in the dog's body. Water aids in digestion, lubricates the eyes, conveys the body's natural electrical currents, is necessary for brain function, and flushes wastes out of the body via the urine.

Dehydration occurs when the dog has not ingested enough water for daily bodily functions. This can happen when the environment is hot, when the dog exercises heavily, or when water is not freely available for drinking. A decrease of 15 percent of the body's water will cause death.

Dehydration can be checked. Pinch a fold of skin on the back of the dog's neck and lift it slightly away from the body; then let go. The skin on a well-hydrated dog will return to normal immediately; but if the skin remains pinched for a few seconds or more, the dog is potentially dehydrated. Offer the dog more water and call the veterinarian.

> **All the Scoop**
> Contrary to popular belief, many dogs get dehydrated in the winter. Some dogs will not feel the need to drink as much as they do in hot weather, and other dogs may not want to drink extremely cold water from an outside source. People living in cold climates need to watch the outside water bowl as it can freeze over.

Dogs should have free access to water whenever they need it. Water should be offered with meals, before and after crating the dog, and before and after exercise. The urban myth that dogs who are hot and tired should not be offered water until they cool off is wrong; dogs need water after exercising.

I have heard there is a housetraining technique being taught to dog owners that recommends restricting water intake so that the dog doesn't urinate as much as she might normally. This is definitely placing the dog's health in jeopardy and should not be done. Although water need not be placed in the crate with a dog in most situations, if the weather is hot, you can put ice cubes in a bowl and place it in with her.

Photo by Mary Fish Arango

Your dog should have access to water.

Belly Aches and Other Problems

Dogs, and especially young puppies, may show distress when they don't feel good. Some will go hide, perhaps in the crate or under a corner table, while others will pant, whine, or come to you begging for attention. Housetraining problems are also common when the dog doesn't feel good. Many other veterinary and health-related issues can affect the housetraining process.

It is very important to recognize that breaks in housetraining caused by physical issues are not training problems; they are health problems. A dog with a urinary tract infection is not urinating in the house on purpose; she doesn't feel good, her urine may burn, and she may not get much warning that she needs to relieve herself.

You need to be able to recognize when something is out of the ordinary with your dog; when something is not right, get your dog to the veterinarian right away. Most dog trainers and behaviorists feel that fully 20 percent of sudden changes in behavior, especially a break in training, are due to physical or mental health-related problems.

Urinary Tract Infection

Urinary Tract Infections (UTIs) are not uncommon, especially in puppies. The veterinarian will need to diagnose it and when he does, usually a short course of antibiotics clears it up. One of the first symptoms is the puppy urinating often, usually with little or no warning. The puppy may not have time to circle or sniff, and she may also urinate in her crate.

Adult dogs can also come down with a UTI. The first symptom is a drastic change in housetraining habits; a well-housetrained dog who never has had an accident may suddenly begin urinating in the house.

Gastrointestinal Upset

A gastrointestinal upset (a stomach ache or problem in the intestinal tract) will cause a change in bowel habits. Diarrhea is very common and can occur after a sudden change in foods, or after the puppy has eaten something she shouldn't have, such as too much grass, cat food, cat feces, or a dead frog in the backyard.

Diarrhea can be serious and can dehydrate a puppy rapidly, especially if combined with vomiting. You should always contact your veterinarian when a puppy has diarrhea.

Step Carefully

Some puppies have a more sensitive gastrointestinal system than others. With some puppies, the tiniest change in foods or treats will cause a problem, while others are regular no matter what. As you get to know your puppy, you'll find out what causes problems and then know how to react.

Diseases That Can Upset Housetraining

There are several diseases that can challenge your housetraining efforts or that can cause a well-housetrained dog to break housetraining. Although most dogs will live their lives without one of these diseases, they are common enough that you should be aware of them.

One of the first symptoms of diabetes is an increased thirst; the dog will crave water often. That, of course, means that he will also be urinating more often and may have accidents in the house because he cannot hold it as long.

Dogs with adrenal gland diseases, either Cushing's (excessive adrenal gland secretions) or Addison's (too little adrenal gland secretions) may also drink significant amounts of water and urinate more frequently than normal.

One symptom of kidney disease may also be excessive thirst and urination, but the opposite may also be true; the dog may stop drinking and therefore urinate very little.

> **Let's Get Physical**
>
> Internal parasites such as roundworms, tapeworms, hook worms, and whip worms can get established in the intestinal tract, irritate it, and cause diarrhea. Although some worms may be seen in the feces, diagnosis is usually made through fecal tests.

Inflammatory Bowel Disease (IBD) can cause vomiting, diarrhea, and weight loss. This chronic disease can often be maintained with diet and medication, but one sign that it is flaring up is usually soft feces or very watery, frequent diarrhea, usually with a break in housetraining. One cause of IBD is an allergy to one or more foods.

Food allergies can also lead to gastrointestinal upset, diarrhea, and a potential mess in the house. If your dog is allergic to one or more ingredient in his food, he may lick his paws, chew at his skin at the base of his tail, and have diarrhea.

You shouldn't assume your dog is suffering from a life-threatening illness just because he's had a housetraining accident. However, it is important that you know your dog. Learn what is normal for him, both in his eating and drinking habits and in his elimination habits. Changes in elimination you should watch for include straining, change in frequency, change in amounts of urine or feces, diarrhea, or blood in the urine or feces. When you see a change, talk to your veterinarian.

Medications Can Mess Up Housetraining

Your veterinarian may recommend a medication to treat a problem for your dog, but sometimes those medications can have side-effects. Some of those side-effects can upset your dog's housetraining habits.

If your dog is given a cortisone or cortisone-related medication, she may begin urinating much more frequently and may not be able to make it out of the house in time. The most common of these drugs is Prednisone, but there are others that cause the same problems.

Some of the drugs given to eliminate internal parasites might, along with the treatment itself, cause diarrhea. Some may also cause an upset stomach.

When your dog is given or prescribed any medications, it's always wise to ask your veterinarian if there are any known side-effects. Not only will this help should there be any urinary or gastrointestinal side-effects, but this knowledge will enable you to watch your dog better and get her back to the veterinarian should there be any dangerous problems.

The Least You Need to Know

- ◆ Digestion doesn't have to be mysterious, and understanding it can help explain the elimination processes.

- ◆ What you feed your dog, as well as when you feed him, can either aid or sabotage your housetraining efforts.

- ◆ Water is essential to life, and your dog needs access to clean water.

- ◆ Several diseases, parasites, and medications can interrupt your dog's housetraining habits.

Establishing a Housetraining Schedule

In This Chapter

- Dogs thrive on (and need) a regular routine
- Setting up housetraining schedules
- Coping with changes to the schedule
- The routine will change over time

People vary in their need for a regular routine. Some people enjoy knowing what will happen day after day; they like their life well ordered and routine. Others thrive on change and like the challenge of not knowing what will happen from moment to moment. Although some adult dogs can cope with a more adventurous owner, most dogs, and especially puppies in training, need a well-ordered routine.

Dogs learn through repetition. When something happens over and over again, and produces the same results each time, they learn and remember what they've learned. Repetition works best when used in a routine or on a schedule. This schedule can work for us, too, as we train dogs. We know that dogs must relieve themselves at certain times, such as after eating. By knowing this, and planning mealtimes, we can then make sure the dog gets outside after each meal.

Dogs Are Creatures of Habit

Dog behavior and training, like many other professions, is in a constant state of change. We are continually learning why dogs do things as they do, and it's been a fascinating journey of discovery. However, we still don't understand why all canines are such creatures of habit. Gray Wolves in the wilds of Alaska, Red Wolves in the mountains of Mexico, African Cape Hunting Dogs, feral dogs in the streets of India, and the dog at your feet may all have different habits and time schedules but they all tend to follow a schedule of some kind. And we don't know why. However, just because we don't know why doesn't mean we can't use this tendency to our advantage.

Almost all creatures are born (or hatched or created) with some instincts. Instincts are those behaviors that are not learned but instead are hard-wired into the animal. Puppies, for example, when first born will move toward their mother's warmth, root around for her nipple, and will then suckle. A newborn puppy hasn't been taught how to do this; this is an instinctive behavior she was born with. I also mentioned earlier in the book the puppy's instinct to keep her bed clean; this isn't learned but instead is simply a part of the puppy.

Habits, however, are learned. These are behaviors that are repeated often enough to become learned by the animal, and then become automatic and effortless. In most cases, when a habit is well learned, it also requires little thought. Smokers, for example, often say they don't think about having a cigarette at certain times, like after a meal; they just do it. That's why breaking a habit can be so difficult.

Step Carefully

Although habits are easy to create because they just require repetition, timing, and reward, they can be very difficult to break. That requires a desire for change, motivation for change, considerable thought, and often a change in timing. Plus there must be a reward for making the change. Therefore, be careful what habits you teach your dog as they can be even harder to unteach.

Let's look at a fairly common dog-behavior problem: jumping on people. Dogs jump up on people because the dog wants to greet the person face to face. That's instinct—a natural way that puppies greet adult dogs—they lick the adult dog's face or muzzle. Dogs don't jump on us to harm us; they don't realize that jumping on people can ruin clothes, knock people down, or scratch our skin.

There are many techniques available to dog owners to correct this problem—such as kneeing the dog in the chest or grabbing his front paws—and few of these work long term. Why? Because these techniques are corrections and do not address why the dog jumps up. He wants (and needs) to greet people so that they will pay attention to him just as an adult dog would had he greeted the adult dog correctly—licking the muzzle. However, if the dog is taught to sit while people lean down to greet him, he then has no need to jump because the people are going to him to satisfy his need for attention from them. When he is helped to sit for petting for a period of time (several weeks), then the sit for petting becomes a habit and the jumping behavior will disappear as it is no longer needed.

We are going to use the dog's ability to form habits to help with his housetraining. By establishing a daily routine and sticking to that schedule as closely as possible for several months, you will help your dog create some habits that will make him a reliable and well-housetrained dog.

A Schedule for the Owner at Home During the Day

If you're at home during the day, it's easy to set up a schedule; what can be tough is keeping it. I say that because I work at home and I know how easy it is to become distracted, either by a new chore, a visit from a neighbor, or a last-minute dash to the store. This can be even harder if you've got kids at home;

children and their activities can be a huge distraction and disruption. However, your dog will not need this strict housetraining schedule forever; but it is important right now.

Photo by Mary Fish Arango

Dogs thrive on a regular schedule. This can aid tremendously in your training.

First of all, list the things you do with your dog and when you normally do them. When do you brush the dog? When do you play with her the most? When does she have her meals? At what time do you walk her? Jot these things and times down on a piece of paper.

Now, you also know your puppy needs to relieve himself after each meal, after waking up from a nap, immediately after getting up in the morning, and last thing before you go to bed at night. He will also need to go outside after an energetic play session. When do those things normally happen? Jot down each item and the times.

Take all of these items and put them in order, timewise, from the first thing your puppy needs to do in the morning after you wake up (go outside) to the last thing at night before you go to bed (go outside!).

Now, list all of your commitments. When do the kids get up? When do they need to leave for school? When do they get home? Does Junior have football practice? When does it begin and end? Does Daughter have a volleyball game? When does Dad or Mom get home and when is dinner usually served? List all of these things and put them in time order.

> **Step Carefully**
>
> If you take your dog outside and she doesn't relieve herself, don't bring her back inside and allow her to have free run of the house. She may just decide to do it inside. Instead, toss the ball around the yard; get her moving, because most puppies have to relieve themselves after exercise.

Now combine your lists. It may shock you; you may not realize how much is involved in each day but do

it anyway. This daily schedule can vary slightly—
Junior may have football only 3 days a week, for
example—but as much as possible of the dog's
schedule needs to remain the same. Remember, we
need to build habits and that requires consistent
repetition.

A partial schedule for the owner of a young puppy
(three to five months old) who's at home during the
day might look like this:

◆ 6:30–6:45 A.M.: Dad is up first and takes
   Puppy outside. Puppy goes, is praised, and is
   brought back inside. Dad puts Puppy in bed
   with Junior.

◆ 7:00–7:45 A.M.: Mom gets up. Gets the kids
   up and feeds Puppy.

◆ 7:45–8:00 A.M.: Puppy goes outside by
   himself while Mom is busy getting the kids
   ready for school.

◆ 8:00–8:45 A.M.: Mom plays with Puppy outside, brushes him, practices some obedience
   training, tosses the ball a few times, and asks
   Puppy to relieve himself. He's praised when
   he does.

◆ 8:45–9:30 A.M.: Puppy follows Mom from
   room to room while she's doing housework
   and chores. He's not allowed to go off on his
   own in the house.

◆ 9:30–11:00 A.M.: Puppy goes outside to
   relieve himself and then is crated while Mom
   runs errands.

◆ 11:00–12:00 noon: Puppy goes outside as soon as Mom gets home; is praised for relieving himself, and then is left outside while Mom answers e-mails, returns phone calls, and is otherwise occupied.

The schedule should give each member of the family time for his or her own needs, yet fulfilling the puppy's needs, too. Your schedule would be different, of course. Any schedule I create would not work for you; you need to establish your own.

A Schedule for the Owner Away from Home

If you're not at home during the day, the preceding schedule will not suit your needs at all. So, just as we did in the previous section, grab a pen and some paper and jot down all of your daily time commitments. Ask your family to help with all of theirs. Don't forget volunteer work, sports, activities with friends, and time for shopping.

Take all of those commitments and list them in order by time, beginning from the moment the first person in the family gets up in the morning. Don't be shocked by the length of the list; most families are busier than they think they are!

Now make up a separate list for your puppy. List all the times she needs to go outside, when she goes for her walk, her playtimes, and mealtimes. When do you practice her training and when do you brush her?

Combine these with your commitments. Here is your tentative schedule. Now that you see it on paper, though, you can streamline it, drop a few things that aren't important at the moment, and assign times for family members to assist with the puppy.

Here's a partial schedule for the owner away from home most of the day:

◆ 6:00–6:15 A.M.: Dad gets up first, takes the puppy outside, praises her for relieving herself, and puts the puppy in bed with Junior.

◆ 6:45–7:15 A.M.: Mom gets up, gets the kids up, fixes everyone breakfast, and feeds the puppy.

◆ 7:15–7:45 A.M.: Junior plays with the puppy outside, tossing the ball, playing hide and seek, and making sure the puppy gets a chance to run and play.

◆ 7:45–8:00 A.M.: Mom asks Puppy to relieve herself, brings her inside, and lets her follow her around the house as she gets stuff done.

◆ 8:00 A.M.: Puppy is crated with a food-dispensing toy and Mom leaves for work.

◆ 10:00–10:45 A.M.: A neighbor, Grandma, comes over, lets Puppy out of the crate, and takes her outside. She asks her to relieve herself, praises her when she goes, and then tosses her ball. When she's tired, she cuddles with her, rubs her tummy, and then asks her to relieve herself again. She then puts her back in her crate.

◆ 12:00 noon–12:45 P.M.: Dad comes home for lunch, lets Puppy outside, and praises her for relieving herself. Puppy is in the house with Dad while Dad eats lunch. Puppy is left outside in the yard in a safe area (perhaps the fenced in backyard or a dog run) when Dad returns to work.

This schedule, like the first one, would combine the puppy's needs with the family members' commitments.

Making a Schedule Work

A schedule will work only if it takes into account everyone's needs—family members and the dog. Therefore everyone in the family should be involved in creating the schedule. If one person makes the schedule and other family members are unhappy, there will be bad feelings and people are less likely to adhere to the schedule. However, if everyone has some input, people are more likely to abide by the decisions made to create it.

Making the schedule will probably require some compromises. Perhaps Junior will need to come home from practice a few minutes early on Tuesday and Thursday to make sure Puppy gets outside in time to prevent accidents, and Daughter can come home a few minutes early on Monday and Wednesday.

The schedule you design should work for you and your family as well as your dog.

All the Scoop

Keep in mind, dogs are not the only ones who appreciate positive reinforcements. If a family member remembers a commitment to the dog, or goes out of the way to help stick to the schedule, praise that effort! Verbal praise, a hug, and a cookie (for kids and adults!) will go a long way to making that person feel appreciated.

Photo by Mary Fish Arango

Once the schedule has been created, post it in a few different places—perhaps in each bathroom, in each kid's room, and on the refrigerator. Each person's commitment can be highlighted in a different color. At breakfast, if the family eats together, they can review the day's schedule.

It is important that each family member understand that his or her commitment to the dog is exactly that—a commitment. Dashing off to go shopping with friends after school instead of coming home to take care of the dog is not allowed. A commitment cannot be disregarded unless the one who is supposed to do something can ask someone else to do it for him. So if Daughter wants to go shopping, she can do that if Junior agrees to come home earlier than he had planned. After all, the dog has no say in the matter!

Over time, the schedule will become routine, both for the people following it and for the dog. As it becomes routine, it will also become easier to follow because it will become habit.

When the Unexpected Happens

Even with the best planning, sometimes the unexpected will occur and someone will not be able to get home on time. Obviously, it's best that the dog not be ignored or left waiting too long. If he learns to relieve himself in his crate, that instinct to keep his bed clean may be lost. That can create a great deal of difficulty in housetraining him.

The best solution is to make sure ahead of time that someone you trust has a house key and can get in to let your puppy outside on time. If you have a neighbor who's often at home, perhaps a trusted teenager who will love to play ball with the dog or a senior citizen who enjoys cuddling with the puppy, that will work. Just give them a call when you've found out your schedule has changed and ask them to go over and let the puppy outside.

If an accident has happened before you get home, do not get mad at the puppy. If the schedule was changed, it's not his fault. Just get him outside and then come back in and clean it up. And try not to let it happen again.

The Schedule Will Change as You Use It

As your puppy grows up, or as your dog learns the housetraining routine, the schedule will change and evolve. A 3-month-old puppy may need to go outside every 2 hours during the day, but a 12-month-old dog should be able to wait for 4 hours before needing to go.

However, there is no timetable as to when this will happen; each dog is an individual. You may just find that on those days when you're at home with the dog, you will ask him if he needs to go outside and he won't need to go. And then he won't have any accidents, either. It will happen gradually.

Let's Get Physical

Dogs do not mature at a steady rate. Their physical and emotional growth may surge ahead at a tremendous rate and then seem to stall. Don't compare dogs, either. All have their own, individual timetable of maturity. Don't worry; this is normal and eventually all dogs do grow up.

It's important that you let your dog make these changes; don't force them on him. If you try to make him fit into a particular schedule that doesn't suit him, there will be accidents. This training is all about preventing accidents, not forcing them to happen.

The Least You Need to Know

- ◆ Dogs are born with certain instincts, but habits are learned through repetition and rewards.

- ◆ The housetraining builds certain habits the dog will then use for the rest of his life.

- ◆ Schedules are unique to each family and dog but help teach the dog good habits.

- ◆ The schedule will change over time but the dog should initiate the changes, not the owner.

Housetraining the Dog Who Has a Yard

In This Chapter

◆ Setting goals

◆ Showing your dog what to do

◆ Supervising the dog in the house

◆ Solving problems

Although many dogs today live in apartments and condominiums, the single-family home or duplex with an attached yard is still the most common home for families with dogs. The yard is often a focal point for the family, especially in good weather. The children play in the yard, the family cooks outside and eats at the picnic table, and guests relax in the evening twilight. Luckily, having the family dog relieve himself somewhere in the yard doesn't have to spoil those family activities.

Establishing Goals

Before you begin the housetraining process, think about what you want your dog to know and to do. What do you want to be the end result of this training? Establishing some goals, and then keeping those goals foremost, will help guide your training efforts. First and foremost should be the idea of teaching your dog where he should relieve himself, and that's outside. The second goal on your list is teaching the dog that he is not to relieve himself in the house. That includes, of course, that he's not allowed to relieve himself in his crate, either. In addition, we talked in Chapter 2 about teaching your dog a verbal command that means, "Relieve yourself now."

But what about some other goals? Do you want the dog to learn how to go in and out through a doggy door? Make sure the doggy door is installed and your dog is familiar with it prior to beginning this training. (Chapter 2 discusses doggy doors, including introducing the dog to the door.) If you don't have a doggy door, should one of your goals be to teach your dog to tell you in some manner that he needs to go outside?

What else is important to you? Do you want him to relieve himself in a specific area of the backyard or can he have the whole yard? Do you want him to relieve himself in the grass and not on the concrete patio? In the next section, we'll discuss choosing the spot, but thinking about where you want him to relieve himself is definitely a part of establishing goals.

> **Step Carefully**
>
> Think carefully about your goals. Make sure you will be happy with the results, as these are guiding your training efforts. Plus, make sure the goals are reasonable and attainable. Once you've established those goals, write them down and post them where you will see them often.

Once you have decided on some goals, write them down and post them in a conspicuous spot; the refrigerator door is good. Keep those goals in front of you so you see them often. Not only will this keep them fresh in your mind, but at those moments when training seems slow or frustrating, the goals will keep you focused on the end result—a well-housetrained dog.

Choosing the Right Spot

As you're reading this section, let's go out in your yard. Where do you want your dog to relieve herself? Choose wisely now because once you teach her to go in this spot, changing it later is very difficult.

Make sure the spot is large enough for your dog to move around when she's full grown. She should also have easy access to the spot. Ideally, it's an area where the family children don't play and away from the family's picnic table. The area should be within easy reach of the hose as you will need to wash it down often to keep the spot clean and the urine smell under control.

This spot can be pea gravel (rounded gravel, not sharp gravel that's uncomfortable on the paws), shredded bark, dirt, sand, or grass. No matter what the surface is, you need to be able to clean it. If there is pea gravel, shredded bark, sand, or dirt, you will be scooping up some of that substrate as you scoop feces, and so you may need to replenish it every few months. If the spot is grass, the dog's urine may kill it and you'll need to soak, fertilize, and reseed that spot often.

Photo by Mary Fish Arango

Where in the yard do you want the dog to relieve herself?

If the spot is one area in a large yard and you want the dog to stay within this smaller space, then put up a temporary fence to partially enclose it. A small plastic fence can divide the "potty area" from the rest of the yard; it can serve as a visual marker for your dog. Just make sure your dog still has easy access to this area.

Teaching Your Dog

In the previous chapters, I helped you build the foundation of skills you and your dog will need to teach him. In this chapter, we're going to put it all together.

In Chapter 2, I talked about how to teach your dog to tell you when he needs to go outside, so go ahead and review that right now as that will be important to this training. You can have one command that means, "Go outside," and one that means, "Relieve yourself." Use the Go Outside command as you head for the door to go out, or as you send the dog through the doggy door. Use the command to relieve himself (I used the example, "Get busy!") once he's outside in the correct spot.

> **All the Scoop**
>
> As you walk to the door, ask your dog in a happy tone of voice, "Do you have to go outside? Huh? Do you?" Your dog is going to respond to that voice happily and most likely will wag his tail, wiggle, or dance. Praise him for that response.

If you haven't introduced your dog to his crate yet, do that now, too. (Chapter 3 will work you through the process.) Using the crate will help you immensely as your dog learns his new housetraining skills.

Restricting His Freedom

As you begin housetraining your dog, get used to having a canine shadow. Your dog should be with you, by your side or in the room with you, so that you can supervise him. If you are too busy and cannot watch him, he needs to be in his crate or outside in a safe area. If he's in his crate, just keep a running tab on how long he's been in the crate. The crate is not a storage box for the dog; he can be in for a few minutes at a time but definitely not for hours at a time, all day every day.

If your dog likes to sneak away from you, then put him on leash and tuck the handle of the leash in your pocket so you can feel it slide if he tries to pull away.

You can also place baby gates across the hall or block doorways so he can't go off into another room.

With your dog close at hand, you can watch him. If he gets restless, begins sniffing the floor, or begins circling, interrupt him quickly ("Hey! Fido, let's go outside!") and then take him quickly to his spot outside.

Using Your Schedule

In Chapter 5, I discussed different housetraining schedules. Hopefully you created a schedule that will work for you, your family or roommates, and your dog.

Your schedule should be posted in several different prominent places, including the kitchen and the bathrooms, and each person should have a copy of it. When everyone knows what the schedule is and agrees with it, there should be few mistakes.

Everyone should use the schedule as both a daily timetable of what needs to be done and as a reminder. I emphasize the use of a schedule because if it's created correctly (getting the dog outside after sleeping, eating, playing, and on a regular basis) then it will work, and it makes housetraining much easier for both the dog and you.

Taking Your Dog Outside

When the schedule shows your dog should go outside, or when you see your dog sniffing the floor, or when she asks to go outside, go out with her. Do not send the dog outside by herself! When she's outside and you're inside, you cannot teach her. Plus, if you praise her when she comes to the door to come back in, you have not rewarded her for relieving herself but instead for coming to the door. That's not the message you were hoping to convey.

Step Carefully

If you send your dog outside by herself, you have no idea if she's relieved herself or not. She could come inside with a full bladder and then relieve herself on the carpet. Go outside to teach her and to make sure she's completely relieved herself.

So, rain or shine, hot or freezing, go outside with your dog and walk her to the spot where you want her to relieve herself. If she has a tendency to run around, take her out on her leash.

If you're teaching your dog to use the doggy door and began the training introduced in Chapter 2, at this point in training you still need to go outside with her. Even though she may let herself out later, right now you still need to reward her for going outside and you still need to take her to the correct spot. So send her through the doggy door, praise her for that, and then walk her to the correct spot.

Wait for It!

Once you take your dog to his spot, just hold the dog's leash and wait. Hopefully, she will have a full bladder and will go. When she's going, praise her softly, using her command, "Get busy! Good girl to get busy!" But don't make the praise so good that you interrupt her; this is the time to reinforce the idea that the command "Get busy" means to relieve herself.

When she's done, then give her the exuberant praise, "Yeah! What a wonderful puppy to get busy!" Let her know you're really happy that she's relieved herself here and not on the carpet!

Do not play with the dog while you're waiting for her to go. Some dogs learn they can get a free playtime out of this trip outside; you don't want to teach that habit. The last trip out at night, at midnight, is not the time to have your dog decide to play! So instead, this is quiet time. If your dog seems hesitant, walk her around, but don't play with her.

When she's all done and you've praised her, then she can run around, play with you, or catch the ball for a few minutes. This playtime is also a reward.

Photo by Mary Fish Arango

Wait for him to relieve himself and then enthusiastically praise him.

Clean It Up!

Always clean up after your dog has relieved himself, both in your backyard and when out on a walk. If you're out on a walk, you can pick up feces by inverting a plastic bag over your hand, picking up the feces, and then pulling the bag down over it all. Tie a knot in the plastic bag and toss it in the outside trash can.

In your backyard, you can use a plastic bag or one of the commercial products, or you can use a shovel and a rake or a commercially sold pooper scooper.

Urine can be washed down or diluted with water from the hose. In any case, do not allow urine or feces to accumulate. The urine can kill your grass if not diluted with water, or on a hard surface, it will begin to smell as it dries. The feces will attract flies and smell. Accumulated urine or feces will also annoy your neighbors.

In addition, many dogs will not go back to any area with standing urine or feces. It's dirty and they want nothing to do with it. This may seem hard to understand because the smell of earlier urine or feces will signal "potty area" to the dog. But it's just the way dogs are; the smell is okay but the actual wastes are not.

She Can Go Back Inside

Your dog can go back inside the house once she's relieved herself. If she hasn't, then she either stays outside until she goes (and you know that she has) or she goes to her crate and you take her back outside in 15 to 20 minutes.

Do not let your dog have free run of even one room of the house if she hasn't relieved herself. It's much too easy for her to squat and go without you seeing it happen.

Take Her Out and About

Once you have begun to feel comfortable about your housetraining routine, begin taking your dog other places. Go for walks and at some point on your walk, in a safe place, ask her to relieve herself. When she does, praise her! Some dogs get so well housetrained to their own yard they will not go anywhere else, and that can be a big problem later.

Also, ask a good friend or family member if you and your dog can come over to their house for a visit. Once inside, keep your dog on leash, and watch her like a hawk, but let her move around. If she gives some signals that she needs to relieve herself, interrupt her ("Hey! Let's go outside!") and take her out. Once outside, tell her to relieve herself there and praise her.

Dogs do not generalize well. She will not assume that your rules for your house apply to all other inside areas unless you can teach her that's what you mean. Once she's gone to three or four different places and learned that the rules apply to all of them, she will catch on.

Solving Some Common Problems

Many dog owners seem to run into problems while housetraining their dogs. Some of these are easily solved. Here are some training tips to circumvent those problems:

◆ Don't get lazy, rushed, or too busy and send the dog outside by himself; you lose the chance to teach him and he may or may not relieve himself. Take the time and teach him.

◆ Use the vocabulary words you've decided upon. Later, you will enjoy being able to tell your dog to relieve himself on command.

◆ Restrict the dog's freedom in the house. Yes, it's a hassle to set up baby gates and close doors, but it's worth it. Don't let the dog go sneaking off into rooms or behind the sofa. A friend of mine is a professional carpet cleaner. As she says, "You won't like what you find back there!"

◆ Be patient! Many dog owners seem to feel that if their dog is not having any accidents then she is well housetrained. I've had people tell me that their 3-month-old puppy has been housetrained for weeks! While I applaud them for having a three month old puppy who is not having accidents, that just means they have a good schedule set up and they are doing everything right for the puppy to succeed.

The Least You Need to Know

◆ Know what you want to teach your dog, set some goals, and then post those goals in a prominent place.

◆ Restrict your dog's freedom in the house until she's well trained and mentally and physically grown up.

◆ Go outside with your dog, teach him a command to relieve himself, and praise him when he does.

◆ Be patient and set your dog up to succeed. Understand that housetraining, bowel and bladder control, and mental maturity take time.

Chapter 7

Housetraining the City Dog to Go Outside

In This Chapter

◆ Setting goals
◆ Always being ready
◆ Showing your dog what to do
◆ Solving problems

Years ago, potential dog owners were told that the only places where dogs should reside were homes with yards. It was cruel to keep a dog in an apartment, experts said, so many apartment dwellers kept a cat, bird, ferret, or fish, and only dreamed of having a canine companion.

Today, people know better. Dogs are very adaptable and can live in mansions or huts, single-family homes or high-rise apartments. Watch the streets of any big city and you'll see dogs of every size, shape, breed, and mixtures of breeds. It's wonderful! However, housetraining the canine resident of an apartment or condominium can be a little trickier than the dog who has her own yard.

Establishing Goals

Goals can help you focus your training. By thinking about your dog, the housetraining process we've already discussed in previous chapters, and your future with the dog, you can decide on a few goals that can help you stay on track with your dog's training.

Some of the goals you may want to establish will be the same for most dog owners, whether the dog lives in a single-family home or a high-rise apartment. For example, you want the dog to know that he is to relieve himself outside, not inside. (I will talk more about where he should relieve himself later in this chapter.)

> **Step Carefully**
>
> If you have a toy to small-size dog, live in an apartment or condominium, and wish the dog to relieve herself inside (such as in a litter box), then skip this chapter and go to Chapter 8.

Your dog will also need to tell you when he needs to relieve himself and he needs to tell you early enough so you can get down the hall, down the elevator, and outside prior to him actually relieving himself. You will also want to be able to tell him to relieve himself and have him try to do it, even if he has to squeeze out one last drop.

What else is important to you? Is your new dog or puppy going to have to get used to city life while learning housetraining skills? Will he need to be comfortable relieving himself in the noise and bustle of the city or is there a park nearby? You know your neighborhood and city best, so take a look around; what is your dog going to have to face while going out each day?

Once you have set some goals, and discussed these with family members, write them down and post them in a conspicuous place, such as the refrigerator. (Put them right next to the housetraining schedule.) The goals will stay fresh in your mind when you see them often.

Selecting the Right Spot

Choosing the right spot (or spots) for a city dog to relieve herself can be much more complicated than the dog who just needs to go to one corner of the back yard. Not only do you have to take your dog's needs into consideration, but also take into account any rules or regulations of the area where you live.

The first thing you need to take a look at are the rules of your apartment building or condo. You have a dog, so I will assume it's a legally allowed dog and not one that has been smuggled in. Does the management have any rules about where dogs can relieve themselves? If you're lucky, they may have established a dog potty area or a dog play yard.

> ### All the Scoop
>
> In an effort to keep dog owners happy and dog-related problems under control, one large apartment complex in Oceanside, California, built a large, grassy, off-leash dog play yard open only to apartment residents and their dogs. The dogs can exercise off leash, play, and relieve themselves in that yard. That keeps the other grassy areas clean so children can play without fear of stepping in dog feces.

Then ask about your city's laws regarding dogs relieving themselves. Because this has been an ongoing problem in many large cities, most do have some regulations regarding it. New York City will fine dog owners who allow their dogs to relieve themselves on the sidewalks, in any public building, on walls, fences, or stairways. That means not only can the dogs not deposit feces on the sidewalk, but they cannot lift their legs to urinate on a public fence, either. In response, most New Yorkers have their dogs relieve themselves in the gutter right next to the sidewalk, out of traffic but close enough to pick up, or in one of the several dog yards.

Although you need to choose at least one spot close to your building for those times when your dog needs to relieve herself right away, to be a good neighbor, avoid having your dog relieve herself immediately outside the building door. Even if you scoop feces, urine can build up and smell horrible.

A green, grassy area can work as a potty area, as can a vacant lot or a park where dogs are allowed. Find a place close to your building where your dog can legally and safely relieve herself.

Where can your dog safely (and legally) relieve himself? Think about this carefully before you teach him.

With one spot chosen that is quickly accessible at those times when your dog urgently needs to go, you should also choose a few more places. Maybe there is an off-leash dog park within walking distance, or a city park where dogs can walk on leash, or a grassy lot. If these places are all within walking distance, then they can be regular stopping points on your daily walks.

Teaching Your Dog

If your new dog or puppy is not used to city life, you will need to socialize him to the sights, sounds, and smells of his new life as you also teach him the housetraining skills he needs to know. Introduce him as gradually as possible, taking short walks at a time of day when life is quieter, and keep it as positive as possible. Keep some treats in your pocket and pop them in his mouth as he faces new challenges. When he walks over a manhole cover bravely, praise him and give him a treat. When he watches a noisy truck go by and doesn't flinch, praise him and give him a treat. Be careful not to comfort him; that will reinforce his fears. Instead, jolly him and praise him for being so brave!

As you introduce your dog to city life, you can also begin his housetraining. In the first few chapters of this book, I introduced you to most of the skills you will need. In this chapter, I'll show you how to utilize what you've learned.

In Chapter 2, you saw how to teach your dog to let you know when he needs to go outside. If you haven't begun that training yet, go ahead and do it now, as that is going to be an important part of your dog's housetraining. Remember, the question, "Do you have to go outside?" should be asked in a happy tone of voice and means exactly what you ask. Ideally, when you ask your dog if he needs to go outside, he should head toward the door with a wagging tail and excited demeanor. In comparison, the command, "Get busy!" (or "Go potty") means, "Relieve yourself right now."

Step Carefully

If you hug your dog and talk softly to him when he's afraid, he will assume those soft words and the petting are praise for being afraid. You may feel you are comforting him and showing him that you are there for him, but his translation will be very different. To make sure there are no misunderstandings, talk to him as if he's silly for being afraid and praise him for facing city life with confidence.

Hopefully your dog is already familiar with his crate and you are using it to prevent problem behaviors in the house and to give him a safe place to sleep. If you need help with the crate training, go back to Chapter 3 and review that information.

Restricting Her Freedom

During the housetraining process for those living in an apartment or condo, the dog should be with you or in her crate. And in the crate means with the crate door closed; an open door is not confinement at all and still allows the dog to sneak away to have an accident. Plus, when I say, "with you," I mean in the room with you or on leash with the leash handle in your pocket so you can feel it should the dog pull away.

When the dog is with you, she can be supervised so you see when she sniffs the carpet or begins to act a little uncomfortable. When she is with you, you can make sure she isn't sneaking off into another room to get into trouble.

Using Your Schedule

In Chapter 5, I explained how a schedule should work and gave you examples of schedules. If you don't have a schedule yet designed and posted in prominent places in the house, you need to do that right away. The schedule is your best means of getting the dog outside when she needs to go and for preventing accidents inside.

Everyone in the household should understand the schedule, know when they are responsible for getting the dog outside, and be willing to work with the schedule. Unfortunately, if the schedule is not followed and the dog has accidents inside too often, she will learn that she can relieve herself in the house or apartment, thereby building a bad habit that will be very difficult to break.

Get Him Out Quickly

One challenge of living with a dog in an apartment or condo is the issue of getting the dog outside quickly enough to prevent an accident. Most puppies only realize they have to go when relieving themselves is imminent; they have to go *now!*

That means you have to be ready. In the early stages of the housetraining process, keep a leash and collar, a handful of clean-up bags, your coat, shoes, and your keys at the front door. When puppy whines, grab everything (including the puppy) and go! Don't take time to finish reading that page of the newspaper and don't finish dinner; just get the puppy outside. You can praise him for whining or otherwise telling you he needs to go outside as you're getting him there.

Let's Get Physical

If you have a young puppy or a small breed, you can pick up and carry the dog to the outside potty spot, especially if you're worried there might be an accident. Just pick up the dog under the chest and back of the hips—not under the belly where you might compress the bladder!

Your dog will need to get outside more quickly at some times than others. The first trip out in the morning will be very urgent, as will the lunchtime trip out if you've been at work all morning. At these times it's especially important that you are sensitive to your dog's needs. Don't make him wait while you fix a pot of coffee; just get him outside! If he has an accident because you've made him wait, it's your fault, not his.

Wait for It!

When you leave your individual apartment or condo and head toward the stairs or elevator, praise your dog for telling you he needs to go outside, especially if he did tell you through his actions or verbalizations. Emphasize the words, "Go outside!"

Once you're downstairs and away from the stairs or elevator, if you've been carrying your dog or puppy, put him down so he can walk to the place where you want him to relieve himself. This is going to be a part of his life and he needs to learn that he's got to walk to it; there is no immediate relief for an apartment dog!

When he gets to that spot, tell him to relieve himself—"Get busy!" As he does, praise him quietly. He needs the praise but you don't want to interrupt him. When he's done, enthusiastically praise him: "Yeah! Good boy to get busy! Yes, such a wonderful dog!"

Now walk him around, toss his ball a few times, and play with him. Some apartment dogs learn to delay the act of relieving themselves because they then must immediately go back inside. Because most dogs, even city dogs, enjoy being outside, play with him, walk him around, and let him sniff the city squirrels. Let him have a few minutes to play and enjoy the outside. This time outside will also serve as positive reinforcement. Plus, after a little play or a walk, he may have to relieve himself again. Then you will know he's really empty when you both go back inside the building.

Take Her Out and About

When you have begun introducing your new dog or puppy to the sights, sounds, and smells of city life, and you have started the housetraining process, then begin taking your dog out and about a little more. Gradually introduce her to the exciting world around her. Keep the introductions happy and upbeat, and have a handful of treats in your pocket so you can reward good behavior.

All the Scoop

Socialization is a vital part of raising a puppy, and city dogs have a unique opportunity that many other dogs do not have. City dogs can meet a variety of people, hear all kinds of noises, and see sights that dogs living in suburban neighborhoods would never see.

Introduce her to the other places where you want her to be able to relieve herself, one spot at a time, of course. Use her command to relieve herself and praise her enthusiastically when she does.

Part of housetraining is also teaching the dog that she cannot relieve herself in some other specific places. For example, city dogs should not relieve themselves on the sidewalk. If she has to go, and it looks like you will not be able to get her to a better place, move her to the gutter. Block her with your body so cars can see you both, but have her relieve herself in the gutter rather than on the sidewalk.

Invite yourself over to a friend's house and take your dog. Keep her on leash but let her move around. Watch her carefully, and if she starts to sniff suspiciously, stop her and get her outside. She needs to know that she's not allowed to relieve herself inside at all, no matter what house she's in.

Dogs do not generalize well and although she may understand she's not to relieve herself in your apartment and your building, she also needs to know that these rules apply to all inside areas. If there is a pet store nearby, take your dog there. Most pet stores allow—and even encourage—dogs to come visit.

Photo by Mary Fish Arango

The owner of a city dog has responsibilities and restriction other dog owners might not have.

Bagging It!

In Pleasanton, California, if you don't pick up after your dog you can be fined $100 for the first offense and $750 for the fourth and subsequent offenses. In Houston, Texas, dog owners can be fined $500. Most cities have laws regarding the removal of dog waste and the vast majority can (and do) impose fines for dog owners (or walkers) who do not clean up after the dogs under their control.

These laws haven't been created by people who hate dogs; unfortunately, dog owners are the reason for these laws. When a dog owner does not pick up after his or her dog and someone steps in it, or when a park is so fouled that children cannot play in it, then complaints result. Therefore, to prevent additional restrictions on our dogs, it is vitally important that dog owners pick up after their dogs.

There are a variety of ways to do this, from a shovel and rake to a commercial pooper-scooper, and from the plastic bag the newspaper is delivered in to commercially sold plastic bags.

The long time owners of city dogs can discuss the pros and cons of various types of plastic bags, and will, given any excuse! The plastic bags from the newspaper are fine except they may have a hole in them from when the paper was tossed onto concrete in front of the building. The commercial bags may be scented, which is always nice, but some are not large enough. Some commercial products come with a scoop built in while others have a way to seal the bag after it's been used. It doesn't matter what you use; just make sure you clean up after your dog every single time he relieves himself.

Solving Some Common Problems

Housetraining a puppy or new dog in an apartment or condo has some unique challenges for dog owners. The benefit, though, is that owners who take the time to do the training correctly end up with extremely well-trained dogs. Here are some tips to keep in mind:

◆ Many puppies know they have to relieve themselves only once it's imminent; they are not aware enough of their bodies to feel the bladder getting full ahead of time. Then once the bladder is full, the puppy has to go right now, and even seconds count. Luckily, you can often avoid this by sticking to the schedule, getting the puppy outside on time, and then watching the puppy for cues that he may need to go. Watch his body language and learn what he does when he starts to get uncomfortable; then get him outside.

◆ Many apartment owners also allow their dogs to have too much freedom. One woman who lived in a studio apartment told me, "I only have two rooms and a bathroom. How can I restrict her freedom more than that?" Easy! The puppy needs to be close to you, in the room with you, or in her crate. Even a two-room apartment has plenty of room for the puppy to wander off and have an accident.

◆ Pay attention to how much time the dog spends in the crate. If he's in the crate all night, he should not spend all day in the crate, too. Find a neighbor, friend, or commercial dog walker to get the dog outside during the morning and afternoon.

◆ Be patient; housetraining takes time. Remember, you are building good housetraining habits as you wait for the dog to mature both mentally and physically. All of this takes time.

The Least You Need to Know

◆ Decide exactly what you want your dog to learn and then jot down your goals. Post those in a prominent place.

◆ Restrict your dog's freedom in the apartment or condominium until he's well trained and all grown up, mentally and physically.

◆ Have a leash and collar, coat, keys, and clean-up bags at the front door so you can get the dog outside as quickly as possible when she needs to relieve herself.

◆ Be patient. Understand that housetraining your dog requires that you teach him new behaviors that will turn into habits over time.

Housetraining the Indoor-Only Dog

In This Chapter

- Setting goals
- Choosing the box and litter
- Showing your dog what to do
- Solving problems

Ethel Gorman had always had dogs. Dogs had been her companions throughout her childhood and on into adulthood. She raised her kids with dogs, and after the kids grew up and left home, she and her husband always had at least one dog. But then she became a widow and disabled, and she could no longer take a dog for a walk. "I can throw the ball to exercise Schatzie," Gorman said of her miniature Dachshund, "but I can't get him outside so that he can relieve himself." However, a friend referred her to me and we got Schatzie set up with a litter box in the house with a litter that helps keep down odors. Even more important, the little red Dachshund took well to the training.

Litter boxes for dogs are relatively new. Although newspapers have been used for puppies for generations, litter boxes have not, and many dog owners have no idea how to use them. But the training is not difficult and many small dogs take to the boxes quite easily.

Consider This Carefully

Dog litter boxes work very well for situations such as Gorman's. Many senior citizens have had dogs all their lives, and in their golden years they need dogs for affection, companionship, and security. Yet many of those same dog owners have some mobility problems that limit their ability to get around, including getting the dog outside. With a dog litter box, the dog can have a place to relieve himself inside the house.

The box also works well for owners who work long hours and must leave their toy or small dog in the house rather than outside. The litter box is also great for dog owners who live in apartments, condominiums, or big-city high-rises, and those who cannot get the dog to a place where he can relieve himself.

Dog Size

Great Danes produce more urine and feces than do Chihuahuas, obviously. Even Border Collies produce more than Chihuahuas. The size of the dog does have bearing on whether or not you should even consider using a dog litter box. A canine litter box is made to order for toy or small-breed dogs, many of whom are the same size or smaller than a large house cat. The amount of urine and feces produced by these dogs can easily be absorbed by the litter in the box.

However, any dog over about 20 to 25 pounds, 30 pounds tops, is probably pushing the limits of dog litter box. Not only will your home tend to smell like dog urine and feces when you come home, but the dog may have trouble positioning himself in the box. His paws may be in the box but he may be depositing the feces outside of the box.

All the Scoop

Apartment dwellers who have a balcony or porch can use a large, lined box (size dependant upon the size of the dog) with grass sod in it. The sod will need to be replaced weekly, but it does give dogs larger than toy size, or dogs used to relieving themselves outside, a place to go.

Leg Lifters

If your dog is a confirmed leg lifter (on every walk he marks his territory as often as you will allow him), you can still make a dog litter box work. The box will have to be large (a mortar pan instead of a cat litter box) and you'll need to place a wooden stake upright in the middle. This stake will have to be scrubbed often and replaced regularly to keep the smell down, but it will give the leg lifter a place to do what he needs to do.

Unfortunately, some dogs will also just mark the sides of the box, which can cause urine to spill outside the box. Some dog owners have foiled their leg lifters by adding "walls" to the box. They do this by taking the top to an enclosed-style cat litter box and cutting off the top and one side. This leaves three sides surrounding the box, thus keeping the urine in the box should the dog be in the box when he lifts his leg.

Although there are some ways to try to control this, before beginning the training, think about your dog's leg-lifting habits. If he's going to mark outside the box or will take advantage of being allowed to urinate inside by hitting the table legs, then you may not want to pursue this.

Dog Litter Box Concerns

Before you begin training your dog to relieve herself in the house, think about it very carefully. Have you ever been disgusted by cleaning a cat litter box? If you have, don't go any further with this training, because a dog litter box can be even worse. And the dog litter box will have to be cleaned just as often as the cat litter box—twice a day.

Once a dog gets used to relieving herself in the house, it will be difficult to change her habits. If you decide that you no longer want to clean up the box, you'll have a very difficult time changing your dog's mind about where she should relieve herself.

Dog Litter Box Options

The litter box itself should be plastic. A plastic box can be scrubbed to keep it clean whereas a wooden box will absorb odors. Cat litter boxes can be used for small toy breed dogs: tiny Chihuahuas, Yorkies, and Maltese. For those a little bigger, a plastic mortar pan (used to mix concrete, mortar, or grout by hand) from your local hardware store will work better. This pan is larger, has higher sides, and is inexpensive.

There are a variety of other types of litter boxes available, made for cats or dogs, but I have found that many have sides that are too low. The litter gets scratched or pushed out of the box, making a mess, or urine or feces are not contained within the box. But take a look at them before you go shopping (see Appendix A) and see if one might suit your needs.

You can use a variety of materials in the litter box. For generations, newspaper was the choice because just about everyone got the morning or evening paper, and it was inexpensive and easy to use. Newspaper, however, is not really absorbent enough for a dog litter box, and has no odor control at all. Plus, many puppies love to rip up newspaper, making a game of shredding it all over. That can be a problem!

The commercial potty pads are also popular, but I've found that too many puppies feel these are toys rather than a place to relieve themselves. And tearing up these pads is entirely too much fun; it becomes self-rewarding behavior. I prefer to use litter rather than paper or pads.

Cat litters can be used in the dog litter box, although some have a tendency to stick to the hair, coat, and paws and can then be tracked out of the box. You can stop some of this litter from ending up elsewhere in the house by putting a bathroom rug (easily washable) on the floor where the dog steps into and out of the box.

> ### Let's Get Physical
> Clumping cat litters should not be used for puppies or dogs who taste, chew, or eat anything. Because puppies must taste everything, the clumping cat litter can be dangerous. This litter swells to 15 times its size as it absorbs liquid; in the puppy's digestive tract, this can be deadly.

The most common litters include compacted wood pellets, paper pellets, compacted pine shavings, cedar shavings, and corn cob pellets. Choose a litter that you can live with and are willing to pay for on a regular basis (prices vary greatly).

Where to Put the Box?

The box needs to be in an area where it can remain indefinitely. Once you begin training, the box should not be moved, as you're training your dog to go to this spot and this box. If the box moves, the training could very well not move with it!

Photo by Mary Fish Arango

There are several options for the canine litter box. Choose the one that will work best for you.

The training will work best if the box is in a small room, like an unused bathroom, or in an area that can be sectioned off to create a small room. The laundry room can work well. Although some people like to keep the dog in the kitchen when he can't be supervised, I'm not a fan of that room. First of all, when you need the kitchen, all the dog stuff is in the way. Plus, it's too easy for dogs to open cupboards or steal food off the counters. So look for another spot.

The ideal spot will be easy for the dog to access, will have tile or other easy-to-clean flooring (no carpet), and will have good air circulation to keep odors down and the dog cool.

Setting Up the Dog Litter Box

Let your dog watch you set up the litter box and his new area. Using a happy tone of voice, make it exciting: "Wow! What's this?" And let him smell everything. If you're excited about it, he will be, too.

Wash the plastic litter or mortar box well and dry it. Place it in the spot you've decided upon. Put a rubber-backed bathroom carpet at the spot where your dog is most likely to climb in and out of the box. Dump a couple inches of the litter into the box and spread it around so the entire bottom of the box is covered.

> **Step Carefully**
>
> Don't be afraid to improvise if you need to. If you want to channel your dog's access and egress to and from the box, place the box in a large cardboard box with a doorway cut into it. If you don't care where she gets in and goes out, but you want to control her tracking of the litter, put a big beach towel under the box so the dog will step on the towel getting out. Improvise as much as you need to so this works for you and your dog.

If your dog wants to climb into the box and sniff, that's fine; invite him in and praise him. However, if he decides to dig in the litter, eat it, or play with it, discourage him and call him out of the box. Do not correct him—harshly or otherwise—or he may think that the box (or litter) is off-limits.

Setting Up Her Housetraining Room

During the housetraining process, your dog is going to need her own housetraining room for those times when you can't watch her, and especially when she will be left home alone. A couple of sections ago, I mentioned that the litter box needs to be in a small room, like an unused bathroom, or in a place where the room can be divided to create a small area. This will be her housetraining room, for lack of a better name.

Ideally the housetraining room should be big enough for her crate, her litter box, a bowl of water, and that's about it. Don't give her lots of floor space right now; that just provides room for her to relieve herself away from the crate and litter box. She can play later when you come home.

If the room is a small bathroom, close off the room with a baby gate high enough that she can't jump or climb it. Do not close the door; that makes many dogs feel overly confined or claustrophobic. If her room is part of a bigger room, set up the boundaries with an exercise pen.

All the Scoop

Exercise pens are foldable fences. You can find them at pet stores or in online dog-supply catalogs. They come in a variety of sizes and heights. Most are metal, but some are plastic.

Introduce your dog to her new area by feeding her there, first with the exercise pen door open so she can come and go, and then later with the door closed. As with crate training, never let her out of the exercise pen when she's throwing a temper tantrum, crying, barking, or whining.

Teaching Your Dog

Teaching your dog to use the dog litter box is not unlike training your dog to use a specific place outside. And as with teaching your dog to relieve himself outside, you're going to use many of the training skills we've discussed in earlier chapters.

In Chapter 2, I discussed teaching your dog to let you know when he needs to go outside. Going outside isn't important here, but going to his box is. Even though eventually your dog will be going to his box alone, right now you will be going to the box with him so you can teach him and reward him for doing the right thing. So you still need to know when he needs to relieve himself. When you take him to his box, use a happy tone of voice as you walk toward the box: "Hey, good boy! Do you have to go to your box? Good!" When his tail is wagging, you're doing it right!

The crate will be an important housetraining tool with this technique, so if you aren't already using it, go back to Chapter 3 and begin crate training your dog.

Restricting His Freedom

During the housetraining process (which can take several months), the dog needs to be restricted in his movements around the house. It is far too easy for him to sneak behind the sofa and have a quick accident or to go off into the spare bedroom and deposit a pile. When his freedom is restricted, you can watch him and then teach him.

He can be in one of three places during housetraining:

- ◆ **With you.** When he's with you, he is by your side in the room with a baby gate across the door or he's on leash with the leash tucked into your pocket. When he's with you, you must supervise him so that if he needs to relieve himself, you can get him to the box.

- ◆ **In his crate.** When he's going to be unsupervised for a short while, he can be in his crate with the door closed. Keep track of how long he's been in the crate, though. You don't want him to relieve himself in the crate, and if he sleeps in the crate at night, he should only be in the crate for short periods of time during the day.

◆ **In his room.** As was discussed earlier, when he's going to be left too long, he should be in his confined space—his room, with his crate (with the door open) and his litter box.

Your dog's freedom will be increased when he's shown that his training is reliable, and when he's mentally and physically grown up.

Using the Schedule

Chapter 5 explained how to establish a schedule that will work for both you and your dog. If you haven't set up a schedule yet, go ahead and do that. If you have a schedule, post it where everyone in the family can be aware of it.

Go back to Chapter 5 if you need help setting up a schedule. You will use the schedule to make sure your dog gets to the litter box on time, just as other dog owners would take their dog outside. The schedule is just as important for your dog because right now she has no idea what that litter box is for; you have to teach her, and to teach her, you need to get her to the box when she needs to go.

Take Her to the Box

When your dog needs to go to the box (after waking from a nap, after eating or playtimes, or at scheduled times) take her to it. Use the leash snapped to her collar to get her there (don't carry her unless you have caught her in the midst of an accident) as she needs to learn how to walk to the

box. When you get her to the box, help her in and
tell her, "Get busy!"

All the Scoop

If you began training your dog on
newspapers or potty pads, take a
couple of small pieces of the paper and
place them in the dog litter box. These will
help your dog transition to the litter box and
the new litter.

You can use the leash to keep her from jumping out
of the box. Don't jerk the leash or choke her; simply stop her from leaving.

When she does relieve herself, praise her enthusiastically, "Awesome! Good dog to get busy!"
Remember, your praise is what makes this all
worthwhile to your dog, so don't skimp on the
praise and petting.

If she doesn't relieve herself, then she goes into her
crate with the door closed for 15 minutes. Then let
her out, leash her, and invite her back into the box.
Repeat until she relieves herself and you can praise
her.

Keep the Box Clean!

The dog's litter box must be kept clean. Ideally,
if you can remove clumps of urine and feces after
each time the dog has relieved herself, that would
be perfect. However, you aren't living your life

to work as a maid for your dog, so that is usually unreasonable. However, the box should be scooped a minimum of twice a day.

Photo by Mary Fish Arango

Use the leash to take your dog to the box even though the box is inside; the leash still gives you some control.

You can use a large cat litter scoop for this. I prefer the metal ones about 4 to 5 inches wide with a deep scoop. It's easier and quicker to use this large scoop rather than a much-smaller plastic one. The clumps of urine and feces can then be deposited into a diaper pail lined with a plastic trash bag. Every other day or so, the trash bag can be knotted and taken outside to the trash or dumpster.

Depending upon your dog, his size, and how strong his urine and feces are, you may need to completely change the litter once or twice a week. At those times you should scrub and dry the box prior to refilling it with litter. At the same time, you can launder the rug or towel under the box.

Cleanliness is very important. If the box smells bad and if urine and feces build up in the box, your dog will relieve himself elsewhere, even if restricted. He may decide to go in his crate or in his water bowl. Although that sounds disgusting, it will be your fault because his box hasn't been kept clean.

Solving Common Problems

This is an easy way to housetrain an inside-only dog, but a few people have run into some problems. Here are a few of the most common ones and their solutions:

◆ **Establish a housetraining room for the dog.** Many owners seem to feel that once the dog has relieved himself in the litter box, he will go back to it from anywhere in the house anytime he needs to relieve himself. He will, eventually, but that training takes time. You need to build a habit, and as you do that, you must make sure the dog does relieve himself in the box—hence, the small housetraining room and the need to walk the dog to the box on leash.

◆ **Use the leash to keep the dog in the box.** You don't want your dog to turn potty time into a game. Without a leash, he can jump out of the box, you'll need to catch him to put him back, and he can jump out again. That's a game. Instead, use the leash to keep him in the box.

◆ **Keep her inside.** Don't take the dog outside to relieve herself until this process is well started. She can learn to go in both places, but teach one at a time so you don't confuse her.

◆ **Restrict her freedom.** I know it's hard to keep a dog restricted, but it's important that you do so. We're using her instinct to keep her bed and living space clean to do this housetraining, and if she has too much room, she may not go to the box. So keep her in her crate, in her housetraining room, or on leash with you.

◆ **Keep the box clean.** Many dogs will refuse to use a dirty box as they don't want to step in urine or feces. Scoop the box at least twice a day and clean the box regularly.

◆ **Do not ask the dog and cat to share a box.** This is asking too much of both pets. The cat would probably stop using the box very quickly and until the cat stopped using the box, the dog would probably be eating the cat's feces.

The Least You Need to Know

◆ Consider all the aspects of this training before you decide to do it. It's hard to stop a dog from relieving himself in the house once he's been taught to do it.

◆ Decide what box and litter you want to use and pick some up. Decide where the box will be located. Keep the box and litter very clean.

◆ Use the leash to make sure the dog goes to the box when he needs to relieve himself.

◆ Restrict the dog's freedom as she learns the process. She should be in her crate, in her housetraining area, or on leash with you.

Chapter 9

Troubleshooting Your Housetraining Efforts

In This Chapter

◆ Identifying problems

◆ Looking at the causes of problems

◆ Working toward solutions

◆ Keeping things simple and doable

Housetraining is one of those subjects that seems to invite people to offer advice. Mention to any dog owners (or anyone who has known someone who ever owned a dog) that you're in the process of housetraining your dog, and they will give you detailed instructions that are sure to be better than anyone else's!

Unfortunately, when dog owners listen to all this well-meant advice, and then change their training to follow it, confusion results. The owner will have a hard time following through because the training technique might be very different, and the dog will not understand what's expected of him.

It's very important to follow through on your training. As I tell my training-class students, "You trusted me enough to come to me for help; now trust me enough to help you." Smile at the people offering you advice, and then continue as you began.

Problems Will Arise

Unfortunately, our dogs cannot yet read this book and so they don't understand how simple housetraining can be. Sometimes dogs get confused and make mistakes. And then often owners don't understand, either, and the dog responds in kind. A recently adopted dog may never have been housetrained, or was badly trained. Mistakes happen and housetraining problems can occur.

Let's take a look at some common mistakes. All of these dogs and owners were in my training classes, although names are not mentioned so that no one is embarrassed.

"When anyone reaches toward my puppy, she rolls over and pees on herself. Why?"

Although the puppy is urinating, this isn't a housetraining issue. Submissive urination is the puppy's way of showing her submission to older dogs and people; she's saying, "I'm just a baby and you're bigger and stronger. Please don't hurt me."

If you get angry and yell at her, this behavior will only get worse. She is using the only language she has to show her submission, and if you get angry, she won't understand. She will only get more stressed.

So stop getting angry immediately. Stop reaching toward her, too. Instead, ask her to come to you, praise her, and offer her a treat when she doesn't urinate. For the time being (a few days or maybe even a couple of weeks) don't even reach out to her when she comes to you. You can pet her when she touches you first, though—just don't reach that big scary hand of yours toward her!

It won't hurt to enroll her in a basic obedience class, either. You can learn how to teach her, and she will gain some confidence as she learns. Just keep the training structured yet fun.

If you keep things calm and gentle, she will outgrow this. It only continues on into adulthood when a dog is very shy and submissive, or in the cases when a dog is shy and has been hurt.

All the Scoop

If you have a dog who is a submissive urinator, greet that dog outside. You will be less likely to get angry because it's not a problem if she leaks out there.

"My dog has used both the litter box and the housetraining pads but refuses to go back to the same spot."

I'm assuming you have tried both the pads and box because you were trying to get the dog back to the same spot. Right now, just pick one: box or pads.

Don't continue to change products or techniques or your dog will be even more confused.

Many dogs dislike relieving themselves in a spot that is dirty. So if he has already soiled the pad or box, he won't go back to it until it's cleaned. That means you have to clean it often, but you can hardly blame him for that.

Now, you have to take his training back several steps and build some reliability. Re-read Chapter 8, and follow the instructions for teaching an inside dog, including making a small housetraining area for him. Make sure you praise him enthusiastically when he relieves himself where he should.

"My dog is a leg lifter. Can he be housetrained so he can be inside?"

Maybe. Unfortunately, I can't make any promises. Some male leg lifters are willing to forego their habit so they can be inside with you. Others are so focused on marking the world, they don't care. However, you can certainly try to make him an inside companion.

First of all, if he isn't neutered, have that done. Neutering is known to help more than 60 percent of leg lifters. Then, begin his housetraining as if he's an 8-week-old puppy. He is either outside, in his crate, or with you. When he's with you, he's on leash with the leash tucked in your pocket so you feel it should he pull away.

Get a black light and scrub all the urine spots you find. Clean with a cleaner made especially for dog urine.

When you see him begin to sniff any vertical object, stop him sharply: "Hey! Don't you even think about it!"

Do not let him have free run of the house for several months. Yes, months. It takes time to break a bad habit. And even then, keep him in the room with you (off leash) for a while, gradually giving him more freedom.

Out on your walks, start cutting down on his leg-lifting there, too. He has no need to go through life marking everything. It's rude and dirty. He's allowed to urinate when you give him permission to, at the beginning of the walk and midway through the walk. Otherwise, no leg-lifting.

> ### Step Carefully
> Some dog owners seem to think that male dogs have to lift their leg to urinate, but that's not at all true. Leg-lifting is marking territory; it's the dog's way of saying, "I was here and I'm this tall!" When another dog marks over that, the new dog is saying, "Ha ha! I was here last and covered up your scent." It's a game of one-upmanship!

Enroll the problem leg lifter in a basic obedience class. Even if you attended a puppy class with him when he was younger, get him into a basic class now. You need to teach him that you can set some rules that he's expected to follow. The training should be fun, so you both want to do it, but you should also be in charge.

Photo by Mary Fish Arango

The leg lifter can be annoying outside but a definite problem in the house.

"My new dog, a shepherd mix, was an outside dog in his old home. Can he become an inside dog?"

It's hard to tell whether your dog will ever be comfortable inside. A friend of mine, Peggy, has a Border Collie, Tipper, who worked her sheep on their small farm. When Peggy's husband passed away and she and Tipper moved to a small house, Tipper still didn't want to come inside. He needed to do his job (watching for strangers and chasing away trespassing birds) outside. However, many other dogs have made the move inside very well.

Begin by bringing the dog inside on leash. If he's worried, keep the visit inside very short and take him back outside and praise him for being so brave. Continue until he can be with you for a while and walk with you throughout the house.

The housetraining can proceed as it would for a baby puppy except that when the puppy is crated, your dog would go back outside.

"Sometimes my dog's urine seems very dark and it has such a strong smell I can smell it in the grass outside. What causes this?"

"I think I see flecks of blood in my dog's urine. Is this normal?"

"My dog's feces are kind of slimy looking. What causes that?"

"Every once in a while my dog has diarrhea. Why?"

Changes in the dog's urine or feces can be caused by many different things—from a change of dog food or treats, to raiding the garbage can, to a lack of water, internal parasites, or a serious disease. Any time your dog's urine or feces changes from the normal, call your veterinarian. She may ask you to bring in a fecal sample, or she may want to examine the dog and get a sample of urine or feces there. In any case, don't assume that nothing is wrong and this change will go away; call your veterinarian.

Let's Get Physical

Don't be embarrassed to call your vet to talk about your dog's urine or feces. Many problems can be diagnosed early if attention is paid to those changes. Your vet will be happy you care enough to pay attention.

"We recently adopted an older Bichon Frise who lived with his elderly owner until she passed away. When we brought him home, we realized he had never been housetrained. Help!"

This dog might be a good candidate for litter box training. Because he's already used to relieving himself inside, it might be easier to transition him to the box than it would be to get him outside.

First neuter him, if he isn't already. Get him checked by the veterinarian to make sure he's healthy and has no underlying health concerns.

Then, go to Chapter 8 and begin his training as outlined there. The key will be control. Keep him on leash and close, or in the crate, or in the house-training area with the litter box. Take your time, and be patient and consistent. This will take several months.

Keep in mind as you begin this training that your dog is probably grieving for his departed owner. This can cause behavior changes, moodiness, and depression. But the new household should help to alleviate his grief somewhat, so during the house-training, make time to play with him, groom him, and take him for walks.

Training the older dog can be a challenge, but it's not impossible.

"Our six-year-old dog used to be well house-trained but is now having a lot of accidents."

First of all, was your definition of well housetrained the same as mine? Did he ever have any accidents? Or just had one once in a while? I consider a dog house-trained when he's mentally and physically grown up, and has had no accidents for several months.

If your dog used to have an accident now and then, and now has them more often, he was probably not well housetrained and is now just getting lazy. He's not taking the time to go outside. Begin his house-training all over again, from the beginning, focusing this time on eliminating all accidents.

If your dog was well housetrained and had no accidents at all, then began having many, you will have to find out why. The first stop should be at the veterinarian's clinic. Ask the vet to do a thorough exam, making sure you tell him why so he can focus on that aspect of the dog's health. Many diseases and medications can cause housetraining problems.

If he gets a clean bill of health, then find out what has changed. Is there a new dog? New baby? Did Junior leave for college? Changes that worry the dog can result in housetraining lapses. Once the change is identified, then try to reassure the dog he is still loved, and supervise him closely in the house until he regains his housetraining skills.

"We just moved to a new house and the dog is urinating on the brand new carpet. Help!"

Start your housetraining all over again, as if he were an 8-week-old puppy. Keep him confined and supervise him closely. He just needs to know that the housetraining rules that applied to the old house apply here, too.

"My three-year-old Samoyed seems to drink constantly; she's always thirsty. This means she's constantly going outside to relieve herself, too. Does this mean she's sick?"

Samoyeds have a very thick, warm coat. In a hot climate, these dogs may drink a lot in an effort to stay cool. You may want to have a groomer brush her thoroughly and thin out her coat a little. See if there is a cool place in the back yard or garage that you can set up for her. Some owners of heavy-coated dogs have even gotten a one-room air conditioner to help keep the dogs comfortable in the summer heat.

Unfortunately, there are several serious diseases that can cause severe thirst and excess urination. Talk to your veterinarian and get your dog in for a complete physical.

All the Scoop

Just because you have a brand new house doesn't necessarily mean your dog was the first dog on the carpet; many contractors bring their dogs to work with them. If your dog is doing a lot of sniffing, he may be smelling another dog's scent on the carpet. If in doubt, have a professional carpet cleaner come in to do the carpets.

"Our dog sleeps with us and is fine but at some point during the night she gets off the bed and relieves herself in the bedroom. My husband is first up and is ready to get rid of her."

You could set your alarm and get up before your husband, but that won't solve the housetraining issue. Basically, your dog is not yet housetrained and so needs to spend the night in her crate. She has too much freedom and is not yet ready for it.

If you didn't crate train her when she was younger, she may not be happy about this change but do it anyway. She needs to develop bowel and bladder control so she can hold it all night.

"My dog, a one-year-old Labrador Retriever, goes back to the same spot on the carpet to relieve herself. Otherwise, she's housetrained."

No, she's not. Housetrained, I mean. A dog who is well housetrained is not having accidents in the house. So drop that thought immediately. Your dog is relieving herself in the house and has just focused on that particular spot. My guess is, though, if you got a black light and checked over all your carpet, you would probably find she has more than one spot where she's going.

First of all, hire someone to thoroughly clean your carpets. Make sure you tell them the carpet needs something for dog urine so they use the correct cleaners. If that spot (and the others) have been too badly soaked (a 1-year-old Lab has a good-sized bladder), that section of carpet and padding may need to be removed.

Then begin her housetraining from the very beginning, assuming she knows nothing about your housetraining rules. Keep her close to you, get her outside on a schedule, and crate her to build bladder and bowel control. She is not to have free run of the house for several months.

"My dog won't go outside when it's raining, snowing, or too cold."

So your dog is a good people trainer, huh? She has taught you that she can set the rules. Well, you need to change the rules. She may be a beloved family member, but it's your house and your carpet and she doesn't need to use it as her personal toilet just because the weather is bad.

Some dogs focus on one spot in the carpet while others feel any carpet is the right spot.

First of all, stop making excuses for her bad behavior. I usually find that when the dog is in charge, the owner has a million and one excuses why the dog doesn't behave. It's cold; it's raining; she doesn't like to get her feet wet; her tummy is off; and so forth and so on. As of the moment you read this, no more excuses!

Enroll in a basic obedience class so you can gain some confidence in your abilities to train your dog. Have fun with the training but make sure you are giving the commands, not your dog, and don't make excuses for her bad behavior.

> **All the Scoop**
>
> Training doesn't have to be all serious. Teach your dog some tricks; that's great fun! You'll laugh, your dog will be the center of attention, and yet your dog will still be learning.

Restrict her freedom in the house, and when it's time for your dog to go outside, hook up her leash and take her. Go with her, make sure she relieves herself, and then praise her. If she doesn't relieve herself, she goes into her crate. She stays in the crate and nowhere else for 15 minutes, and then she goes back outside again. She'll catch on.

"My twelve-year-old Golden Retriever has always been well housetrained but is now having accidents—not all the time but once in a while."

Your old girl needs a complete examination from her veterinarian first. Make sure you tell him everything that's been going on, including the housetraining lapses. There are many age-related health issues that can cause sudden or frequent urination.

If her health looks good, then she may be suffering from a form of canine dementia. This often shows up as housetraining lapses, confusion, and sleep disorders. Although there is no cure for this, medications may slow its progression.

"We were told to use a crate for housetraining but our dog relieves himself in the crate. What did we do wrong?"

This is commonly seen in pet store puppies, especially those that get their puppies from puppy mills. The puppies are born in cages at the puppy mills, are in crates or cages when shipped to the stores, and are in cages at the store. The only place the puppy can relieve himself is in the cage.

Unfortunately, this also happens with some otherwise well-meaning breeders. They get too enthusiastic about their breeding program, end up with too many dogs, and the dogs spend too much time in their crates.

Ultimately these dogs need to spend more time in a safe place outside where they can relieve themselves at will. When the dog is brought inside, he needs to stay with you, on leash with the leash in your pocket, so you can watch him and teach him. When he can't stay outside, set him up a housetraining area as discussed in Chapter 8.

But these are not the only causes of a dog relieving himself in the crate. You may be asking him to spend too much time in the crate or he may have an underlying physical reason for this, such as diabetes or a medication he's being given. So take a look at how much time the dog is being asked to spend in the crate, look at his background, and get him checked out by the veterinarian.

Photo by Mary Fish Arango

The dog who relieves himself in the crate may have one of a variety of problems.

"Our female dog is about 10 years old now and has always been well trained. She never had housetraining accidents. But now we've been finding wet spots where she's been sleeping."

Older spayed female dogs often leak some urine when they're in a deep sleep. Don't scold your dog;

she has no control over this. Definitely talk to your veterinarian, though, as there is a medication that can help.

> **Step Carefully**
>
> You can lessen the mess from these leaks by placing a lined (leak resistant) housetraining pad or diaper under the washable blanket where the dog usually sleeps.

"We got a new dog and now our older dog is making housetraining mistakes."

"We recently had a baby and now our dog is making housetraining mistakes."

The reason for both of these problems is probably jealousy. New dogs and new babies tend to gain a lot of our attention. We coo over them, clean up after them, offer them tempting foods, and the older dog looks on, not getting any of that good stuff.

The key is to make sure the older dog gets plenty of one-on-one attention away from the new puppy and new baby. While Mom takes care of the baby or puppy, Dad can take the older dog out for a walk and a session of Frisbee. While the baby is napping and the puppy is in her crate, the older dog can spend time in the living room getting petted, groomed, and cuddled.

At the same time, make sure any spots are cleaned up very well so the smell is gone. Keep a closer-than-normal eye on the older dog and make sure he gets outside regularly. Other than that, as soon as he realizes the new addition isn't a threat to your love and affection, the housetraining should go back to normal.

"My dog doesn't tell me when she needs to go outside."

Teach her to ring some bells. I don't like to teach dogs to bark to go outside because I also hear from far too many owners with problem barkers. But ringing the bells is a fun trick and can serve a useful purpose.

Go to the local craft store and pick up some bells. One to two inches across is a good size. Hang the bells from the doorknob where you want the dog to go outside, making sure the bells are at your dog's nose height.

With your dog by your side, close the door, and then rub the bells with something that smells good to your dog, like hot dogs or cheese. When he sniffs the bells, praise him and give him a bit of the smelly food. When he rings the bells to get a treat, open the door, step outside with him, and give him the treat outside.

Using small training steps like this, continue the training until you can get the dog all the way to his potty spot in the back yard, have him relieve himself, and then hand over the treat, with praise.

When you and your dog can do that, then ask the dog to ring the bells before you open the door. When he can do that, just listen for the bells!

"My tea-cup Toy Poodle has never been well housetrained and my husband is having a fit that the carpets smell."

"I have a teensy Chihuahua just like [name the celebrity] and she is a wonderful pet but she has never been housetrained and I'm not happy about it."

This is a common problem that dog trainers and behaviorists run into all the time. Many of us believe that because the very small dogs make such tiny puddles and piles in the house, it's easier for the owner to clean up. (A big dog makes a big puddle and pile and it's much harder to ignore.) Also, people tend to make more excuses for the small dogs ("Oh, but she's so tiny …").

But there is nothing in the genetic or physical makeup of these small dogs that makes them difficult to housetrain. At one point in our lives, my husband and I had Papillons (a toy breed) and German Shepherd dogs. All of the dogs were trained the same way, including housetraining, and all the dogs were expected to observe a high level of obedience. The Papillons were no more difficult to train than their larger cousins.

So, re-read the book, from Chapter 1 on, and train those tiny dogs. Show the world how clever toy dogs can be!

The Least You Need to Know

- ◆ Toy and small breed dogs are just as capable of learning housetraining skills as are the larger breeds.

- ◆ Dogs may react to changes in the household (a new baby or a new puppy) by breaking housetraining. Help the dog cope with the change as well as retraining the housetraining skills.

- ◆ Housetraining problems occur for a variety of reasons but most are fixable.

- ◆ When housetraining accidents happen unexpectedly, for no apparent reason, call your veterinarian.

- ◆ If you see any changes to your dog's stool or urine, call your veterinarian.

- ◆ Housetraining takes time to change older bad habits, and time to build new habits. Be patient and consistent.

Internet Resources for Dog Owners

Additional Housetraining Resources

Central Dakota Humane Society

Housetraining information for puppies and older dogs.
www.cdhs.net/housetraining_puppies_and_dogs.htm

Greater West Metro Humane Society

Information about housetraining puppies.
www.animalhumanesociety.org/
bhv_housetrainpuppies.asp

Dog Owners Guide

Information about cleaning up after housetraining accidents.
www.canismajor.com/dog/hsetrain.html#clean

Purina Second Nature Housetraining

Dog litter, dog litter boxes, and additional information.
www.doglitter.com/GetPage.aspx?D=
9543015&T=3785401

Drs. Foster & Smith

Pet Education site. Cleaning up after accidents.
www.peteducation.com/article.cfm?cls=2&cat=
1645&articleid=805

Pet Supplies Online

Drs. Foster & Smith

All kinds of supplies, from housetraining aids to dog
foods.
www.drsfostersmith.com

Dog.Com

Dog gifts, toys, and more.
www.dog.com

J-B Wholesale Pet Supplies

Everything a dog owner could ever need.
www.jbpet.com

All Dog Supplies

Dog supplies of all kinds.
www.alldogsupplies.com

Petco Online

Everything the stores have and more.
www.petco.com

PetSmart Online

Everything the stores have and more.
www.petsmart.com

Canine Health

Canine Health Information Center

Information of all kinds regarding dog health.
www.caninehealthinfo.org

Dog Pack.Com

Information about dog health and diseases, and articles about dog food.
www.dogpack.com/health/dogHealth.htm

American Kennel Club Canine Health Foundation

A wealth of information about dogs and their health.
www.akcchf.org

More Dog Food Resources

The Dog Food Project

"How Does Your Dog Food Compare?"
www.dogfoodproject.com/index.php?page=main

Doberdogs.com

Dog food comparison charts. Excellent resource.
www.doberdogs.com

Kibble Ingredients

What is in dry dog foods? By name brand.
www.iei.net/~ebreeden/kibble.html

Second Chance Ranch

Argument against raw foods.
www.secondchanceranch.com/training/raw_meat/
index.html

The Honest Kitchen

The makers of the first raw, dehydrated foods for
dogs and cats.
www.thehonestkitchen.com

Index